AUTOGRAPHED EDITION

Myself-To Date, Irvin S. Cobb

IRVIN S. COBB

THE WORKS OF
IRVIN S. COBB

STICKFULS
(MYSELF—TO DATE)

THE REVIEW OF REVIEWS CORPORATION
Publishers   NEW YORK
PUBLISHED BY ARRANGEMENT WITH GEORGE H. DORAN COMPANY

Acknowledgments are herewith made to
The Saturday Evening Post, McClure's Magazine, Life, The American Magazine and Everybody's Magazine, in which portions of the contents of this book originally appeared.

Myself—To Date. I

TO

THE MEMORIES OF THESE TWO:

CHARLES EMMET VAN LOAN
THOMAS MARTIN O'CONNOR

Myself-To Date, Irvin S. Cobb

CONTENTS

Stickfuls

GETTING SET IN NEW YORK
CHAPTER ONE

The First Stick

Stickfuls

CHAPTER I

The First Stick

LIKE most of the men who break into New York newspaper work I came from the country. Unlike most of them, I waited until I was getting well on toward thirty before I made the break.

I was born and brought up in one of those border-state towns that Northern people call Southern, and far Southern people call Western. When this town had about fifteen thousand inhabitants, and when I had just turned sixteen, being then a lank, gangling youngster, who was getting ready to go off to military school as a preliminary to a college education, a sudden and disastrous shift in the family finances made it imperative for me to make my own living.

I had already had some small experience at earning money for myself. To earn spending money I had delivered newspapers for a few months once and the summer before, during vacation, I had driven an ice wagon, with a darky on the back end to handle the ice, and me perched up front to steer the mules and make change. But the ice business had never appealed to me —you had to get up at three o'clock in the morning, for one thing; so when this shipwreck of the family fortunes occurred I decided right away that, no matter what I became in after life, it would not be an iceman.

I had a chance to read law in the office of a kinsman and I rather liked the prospect. It seemed to me that the lawyers constituted a favored class in our community. Their offices were in a double line of little squatty brick buildings, stretching along a block known as Legal Row; and, so far as I had been able to observe, they never did any harder work than sitting in their offices, with their feet cocked up on their desks, reading leather-backed books—except that in campaign years they made speeches and ran for office. And on pleasant afternoons, along about four o'clock, they would emerge from indoors and gather in groups along the sidewalks under the shade trees, swapping jokes and stories. And often there would be a game of marbles back of somebody's office with a watermelon cutting to follow. I have seen a former Congressman, a future United States Senator, a portly Circuit Judge, and a man who had been a brevet-brigadier in the Confederate Army, all in the same marble game, playing Plumpin' Boston.

The law was a fascinating pursuit—yes; but it might be years before I could earn anything at it, and what I needed was a job that had an immediate pecuniary connection to it. So I scouted round town, and I was just about to land a place in the city passenger office of one of the two railroads at three dollars a week to start on, when one night my father came home and asked me how I would like to be a newspaper man.

It did not take more than a second to

make up my mind, and I know now that the decision of that moment shaped my whole life for me. To be a regular newspaper reporter, with a pad of paper and a pencil in my pocket, going round gathering news items and writing them out to be read, struck me as a much more dignified and important calling than running errands for a railroad company. Besides, I had felt all along that I was not cut out for a commercial career. I had never learned the multiplication table—and never have yet. I get along fairly well up to ten times six, but after that I have to depend on the other fellow's honesty; or else I arrive at the approximate result by a private process of my own, which is reasonably satisfactory, but takes time. At the grammar school I got through Ray's Higher Arithmetic by the simple expedient of doing their Latin for certain of my classmates while they did my problems for me.

On the other hand, I had been the brag composition writer of my class. Algebra was ever an unfathomable mystery, but writing, as we used to say, just came natural to me. When I was fourteen I had prepared an argument for a Friday afternoon debate on the subject, "Resolved, that Columbus deserved more credit for discovering the country than Washington did for saving it," which my parents had regarded as a very fine piece of writing. In the vote on the debate our side lost, but one of the local papers had printed my argument—by request—and quite a lot of people complimented me on it.

Even that far back I had felt that writing was my proper trade. A print shop always had a lure for me. I cannot recall a time when the smell of ink and of print-paper did not draw me; nor a time when the mere sight of a sheet of clean paper failed to arouse in me a desire to make black marks on it. My earliest known photograph shows me, at the tender age of twenty months, lying flat upon my stomach—I could lie flat upon my stomach then—engaged in scribbling upon a sheet of paper with a stub of pencil. Tradition has it that on this occasion, having been dressed in my Sunday best and taken under parental

escort to the photographer's establishment,
I resolutely refused to be interested in the
promise of the officiating functionary that a
little bird was about to come out of the black
box. It would seem that, at that moment, I
cared little for ornithological phenomena.
It is also recorded that I howled, opening
my mouth widely. I am constrained to believe that when, at that age, I opened my
mouth widely I must have looked a good
deal like a detachable rim. Now, my parents did not desire to have an interior view
of me. They knew already that I possessed
superior acoustic qualities, and had no wish
to preserve the revealed aspect of my personal sounding-board with the aid of the
camera's eye. Rather, they longed that I
might be shown with my features com-
posed; for already the Home Beautiful
movement was spreading through America.

But I declined to be beguiled by cajolery,
blandishments, or the prospect of beholding
foolish little birds flying about. I have
been told that I wept unabatedly and whole-
souledly until my mother, remembering a
predilection already evidenced by me, put

into my fingers a scrap of lead-pencil. Immediately I became calm, and a faded photograph which is now treasured in the family archives was a result.

I imagine that I was trying then to draw rather than to write, for I started out to be an artist. As far back as I can remember I drew pictures of sorts. Pictures which I drew at the age of four years old have been preserved. I doubt whether Michael Angelo drew any better at the age of four than I did; and judging by some of his canvasses that I have seen, I am constrained to believe that Rubens, in his maturity, did not know much more about drawing the outlines of the human figure than did I ere I had attained my fifth birthday. One main distinction between us was that I eventually knew enough to quit trying and Rubens never did.

As I said just now, I had grown into boyhood with the smell of printer's ink in my eager young nose. My favorite uncle, for whom I was named and whose especial protegé I was, was a newspaper contributor and he wanted me to grow up to be a newspaperman, too. His literary fancy took a curious two-way turn. When he wasn't doing barbed wire humorous paragraphs he liked to write lugubrious obituaries. Locally, he had no equal in either of these fields. He didn't write for the money there was in it—for he had an income from other sources and I doubt whether he ever earned a hundred dollars, all told, with his pen—but for the love and the joy of creation. He liked to keep me by him when he was writing; he said you couldn't start too soon training a boy for a journalistic career. Before I was out of dresses and into short breeches I had spent many a day in the odorous, cluttered and altogether fascinating atmosphere of the little old print-shop where he turned out his work.

So when my father made the suggestion to me that I might get a job on the same paper which this uncle, now dead and gone, had, in his time, served, I jumped at the prospect. I have never regretted it. I've always known that, whether I succeeded at it or failed at it, newspaper work was the thing on earth for which I best was suited and which best suited me.

So the next morning at eight o'clock—the date was January sixteenth—I went to work as a newspaper reporter. That was nearly thirty years ago, and in one sense or another I have been a newspaper reporter every day ever since; experience has taught me, though, that there never was and never will be a newspaper office just like the one in which I made my start.

The principal owner and virtual head of the establishment was one of the most lovable men that ever lived. Mainly he presided over the business department. When a farmer came in and paid his subscription for the weekly edition—which was two dollars by the year—Boss Jim, as everybody called him, would pitch one dollar into the cash drawer; and then, without a word, he would make for the door. All within sight who could spare the time—bookkeepers, editors, reporters, pressmen, printers, loafers—would trail after him as he led the way to Uncle John's place next door; and there they would line up in a row at the bar while Boss Jim spent the extra dollar on toddies at ten cents apiece. Sometimes this would happen half a dozen times a day.

This shop was a regular happy family. Boss Jim's brother was the editor of the paper, which was an evening paper with a Sunday morning edition. His brother's brother-in-law was the business manager. Two of his sons, two of his nephews and any number of his cousins and his relatives by marriage had jobs of one sort or another about the place. There were several editors, all of whom did reporting after a fashion; but until I joined the staff that January morning there was only one avowed and admitted reporter. He was probably the best man of his inches at gathering news, and the worst at writing it, on the habitable globe. He started every story, big and little, the same way—with the hour of the event's happening. His introductions never varied, but they seemed to give general satisfaction—at least, I never heard any complaint either from the editor or from the public.

If they had only one reporter they had editors to spare. There was a river editor, who handled the steamboat column, one of the most important departments of the paper, and on the side solicited orders from the boats for work out of the job-printing and book-binding departments. There was an exchange editor, a mentally alert but physically indolent man who seemed to live entirely on chewing tobacco and clippings. There was an editorial writer—we were strong on editorials—and there were four elderly men who had a more or less indefinite connection with the paper, writing what pleased them when it pleased them, and being paid mainly in orders for merchandise on merchants who advertised with us. Three of these four were Confederate veterans, and the fourth was a Union veteran, who had drifted in from somewhere up North years before and, finding the climate congenial and the whisky at Uncle John's place unexcelled, had remained ever since—shabby, scholarly, irresponsible, a gentleman drunk or sober—the first real newspaper Bohemian and the only real one

I ever saw. He wrote only when the spirit moved him; but he could write like a house afire. I remember well the day they fished his body out of the river. The theory always was that, being overtaken with fatigue, he went to sleep on the deck of the wharfboat and walked in his sleep.

Also there were several middle-aged gentlemen who used to drop in daily to read the exchanges and swap talk—and wait for Boss Jim to take in a subscription to the weekly. Many a time I have seen the reporter standing up to write his copy, and the exchange editor eating big bites of plug tobacco and clashing his empty shears in a silent fever of impatience, while these visitors occupied the chairs and took turns pawing over the exchanges.

In spite of these things the paper was prosperous. It had no regular advertising solicitor, no regular subscription manager; yet it made money—a good deal of money for those days and that country. The job office and the book bindery ran overtime, and our weekly edition—made up entirely of matter lifted from the daily—had a circulation that covered the Congressional district like a blanket.

In general elections the paper was always rigidly Democratic—the Democratic party could do no wrong and the few Republicans in our section could do no good, and the Democratic ticket was always made up of scholars and patriots, while the occasional Republican nominees were invariably horse-thieves and liars; but in the preliminary races for the Democratic nominations the editorial support was regularly sold to the best bidder. There was very little concealment about this barter of the editorial column and no impropriety. To advocate a Republican's candidacy for office would have destroyed the paper's following overnight, but a fight among Democrats was a different thing—was, in fact, a family affair; and it was perfectly proper to take money for advocating the claims of any candidate whose political orthodoxy was above suspicion. Moreover, it never seemed to impair our influence among the country people. I recall once we pulled through— for an agreed price—a candidate who was opposed by practically all the other papers in the district.

It was into this unique establishment that I was welcomed of a brisk January morning, and such was the atmosphere of the place that inside of half a day I, an embarrassed, nervous boy, felt as much at home as if I had been born and raised there. The editor finished whatever he was doing, and then he opened a drawer and gave me one of those old-fashioned red-cedar pencils with a vein of slate running through its center. He offered me a pad of paper too, but I was already provided in that direction —I had bought a large leather-backed notebook on my way downtown—and then he told me to go out and try to find some items. I remember my bewildered feeling as I buttoned my overcoat round me and stepped out into the wind-blown street. Always before this street had seemed to me fairly to throb with life and movement. Now, all of a sudden, it had become as cold and empty as an open grave. It looked as if nothing ever had happened there; as if nothing ever was going to happen there.

I wandered round in a lost sort of way until I came to the Market Square, where a few hucksters shivered at their stalls under the long open shed. There I got my first item. I would call it a "story" now, regardless of its length; but then all the small grists that came to my mill were "items," and the longer ones were "pieces." Thanks to a sort of photographic gift of mind, which has been my best asset as a reporter, I can still see this my first item just as it appeared in the paper that evening in a column headed Local Notes, sandwiched in between patent-medicine reading notices:

"Cal Evitts, the efficient and popular market master, says there were more rabbits brought to the local market this week than any week this winter. Molly Cottontails sold this morning for ten cents dressed or five cents undressed."

This was the sum total of my literary efforts for this day. During the rest of the day I hung round, absorbing the spirit of the place and at frequent intervals resharpening my red-cedar pencil. It was a fine pencil for sharpening purposes, but a poor one for writing. It made more scratches than marks, but to me it typified my new calling in life, and I valued it accordingly.

On the second morning the editor suggested that I might look round a while for personals. I knew how to set about getting personals. I went to the depot to meet the morning trains and see who got off and who got on and I was at the wharf when the daily packets arrived—one from up the river and one from down; and I dropped in at the principal hotel and copied the list of names on the register. At first I felt a timidity about coming right out and saying that I was a reporter; but, as I knew practically everybody in town, I could presume on my acquaintance to ask people in an off-hand kind of way where they had been and where they were going; and so I got along. By rapid degrees my timidity wore off, but for quite a while I approached strangers in preference to townspeople. Folks whom I knew would laugh when I told them I was a reporter, and I had to suffer a lot of guying.

Nevertheless, I managed to turn in about

two columns of personals a day, and sometimes three. It was good newspaper copy
for a small town, or a large one, either, for
that matter—people like to see their names
in print, except when they have been caught
doing something wrong. Everybody who
traveled at all was good for two personals—
one when he went away and one when he
came back. Pretty soon I learned to im-
prove on the system and make four personals sprout where but two had grown before.
If a man told me he was going to St. Louis
or Memphis on such and such a date, I
entered his name in my notebook twice—
once for immediate use and once for future
reference. I would print one personal, telling that he was going away; one that he had
gone away; one that he was coming back
on such and such a day; and the fourth upon
his return, when I would duly chronicle his
safe arrival.

Meanwhile I was getting acquainted inside the office. I hobnobbed with the press-
man and the printers, most of whom were
fixtures. However, we had our share of
tramp printers—erratic, uncertain, capable

chaps, born spellers most of them, men who had been everywhere and had seen everything, and generally men who had read a lot and remembered what they had read; so that, from reading and travel and observation, they were walking mines of information on all manner of subjects—a strangely attractive type who died out as a class when the linotype machines came in. I disdained to have any dealings with the carrier boys, though some of them were almost as old as I was and had been friends of mine before I attained to the lofty eminence of a reporter's job; and I was accepted on sufferance by the elder statesmen of the editorial room and was soon, in all things, part and parcel of the organization. except when Boss Jim took in a cash weekly subscription and led the march to Uncle John's place. I was too young yet to join that procession.

Gradually my field of operations outside the office widened. The regular reporter handled the routine. He covered the police court—a daily event that was always good for half a column and sometimes more

—the City Hall, the County Courthouse, the two undertakers' establishments, the sheriff's office and the magistrates' offices, the tobacco warehouses, the wagon yards and the livery stables—all the regular news points. So, when I tired of personals as a steady and exclusive literary diet, I set about developing news sources of my own. I began making daily visits to the railroad shops, a place theretofore neglected from the news standpoint, except when something out of the ordinary happened there. I collected gossip and personal notes of the men.

Occasionally, on a particularly busy day when there were a lot of boats in port, the river editor would permit me to help him out. I enjoyed this most of all; it threw me into the fascinating company of the mates and captains and pilots. Plenty of the oldtime antebellum rivermen were still in active service then, and they were a wonderful race too—the more wonderful because they are nearly all gone now. Moreover, the assignment was good for about so many invitations a week to eat meals aboard boats in port. I would eat at the officers' table

and they would stuff me full of strange tales
—some of them true, but most of them
imaginary. I wrote a lot of these tales for
the paper; and, crudely told though they
were, I know they must have been fairly
good stuff. But they frequently got
crowded out. If there was any overset matter the editor would shove my other stuff
aside to make room for my personals; and
from the angle of the small-town editor he
was exactly right.

For the first three weeks of my apprenticeship nothing was said about pay. It had
been understood in a vague kind of way that
I would work for nothing until such time as
my services became sufficiently valuable to
entitle me to wages. At the end of my third
week, on Saturday night as I was leaving
the office, Boss Jim called me back and
pressed some coins into my hand. I could
hardly wait to get outside to count them.
He had given me a dollar and seventy-five
cents. Up until then I had felt a haunting
uncertainty regarding my real status as a
member of the staff, but now all doubt was
gone. The proof lay glittering in the palm

of my hand. I was a regular newspaper reporter on a regular salary. It is my present recollection that I outgrew a suit of comparatively new clothes over Sunday—the vest especially becoming too tight across the chest.

In two months my pay was four dollars a week and I was writing my share of the paper and more. The writing game suited me, and I throve on it and was greedy for more. Seeing how willing to work I was, the principal reporter began letting me cover part of his territory for him. I was glad of the chance, and it gave him more time for sitting in the city marshal's office, and so the arrangement proved highly satisfactory all round. I wrote all sorts of items—court proceedings, trials, crimes, accidents, deaths, notices of the shows that came to the opera house, business changes—even editorial paragraphs of a supposedly humorous nature. I covered the county fair, a big annual event; and I did weddings and political rallies, revival meetings and the openings of new saloons. These last went in as news items, but were paid for as advertisements. I was actually allowed to report a meeting of the city council—which was a thing of such importance that frequently the managing editor himself covered it. I could draw a little and sometimes I illustrated my own yarns with chalk-plate pictures.

As a matter of fact, my prime intention when I started out was eventually to be an illustrator or a cartoonist—preferably a cartoonist; this writing work, as I figured, was merely in the nature of preliminary training in a congenial atmosphere for my real calling. Indeed, before I ever wrote a line for publication I had seen some of my pictures in print. When I was fifteen I sold three or four crude drawings to *Texas Siftings,* a publication long since defunct, and one alleged caricature to a weekly publication in New York, whose very name I have forgotten; anyhow it died years and years ago, so the name doesn't matter. For the caricature I had received the sum of one dollar—the first dollar I ever earned with either pencil or pen. *Texas Siftings* forgot to send me a check. But it ran my

drawings, which was the main consideration with me. At fifteen I wasn't after a fortune. I craved fame.

After a few months, though, as the scope
of my duties broadened, I quit doing chalk-
plates altogether and gradually with lack
of practice I almost entirely lost the knack
of making pictures.

None of my stuff was ever edited except
for spelling; I have never been what you
would call a fancy speller, and as I grow
older it seems to me my spelling is marked
by a more striking individuality all the time.
The editor would correct a few of my more
conspicuous outbursts of originality in the
matter of spelling, but that was as far as
he went. Neither for style nor for syntax
was my copy revised. It went in just as it
was written. In one way this was good for
me and in another way it was decidedly bad.
The freedom of it bred in me the joy of
creation and encouraged me constantly to
keep enlarging the scope of my writings;
but the absence of any editorial discipline
made me careless of results and freakish
and fresh. I was entirely too fresh for my

own good and what I wrote reflected my freshness.

Also, I had the delusion, so common among beginners at the writing trade, that it was bad form to use the same noun twice in the same sentence or the same paragraph; so. if I were writing a story about a cow, I would call her a cow first, and then a female bovine, and then a ruminative quadruped—and so on.

As I went along I began to manifest a natural knack for headlining. Pretty soon I was putting heads not only on my own stuff but on most of the stuff the other reporter wrote. My taste in headlining ran strongly to the startling, and this proved a novelty. I remember one headline of mine that attracted considerable attention.

There was a rather pompous, self-sufficient lawyer in town, one of the old silver-tongued school of orators. With him the paper was at outs politically. Even I, a seventeen-year-old boy, could see through his pretensions and appreciate that he was mostly a large bluff inhabiting a Prince Albert coat. We were taking a slender little wire service then and padding it out in the office to make a front-page column of telegraph. One day there came along a dispatch from the state capital giving a list of delegates who had been appointed by the governor for an irrigation congress out West somewhere. The last name on the list was the name of our champion silver-tongue. I ran the special just as it stood, with this headline over it:

A GOOD JOKE

Will be Found at the Extreme Southern
End of This Dispatch

The town saw the point, and the whole town laughed at it—all except the silver-tongued one. He made statements in public places touching on his intention of taking my young life with his bare hands. I managed to dodge him for a day or two; and then one afternoon just after we had gone to press he walked into the office and started for me, cursing as he came. He had been drinking, I think. One of the old-soldier members of the staff—he had been a captain in the Confederacy—stepped between us. He pulled out a spring-back knife and opened it with a flirt of his thumb. The blade was stained black by much paring of apples and slicing of plug tobacco, but it was plenty long, and plenty sharp, too, I guess. He was a small, quiet, grizzled man.

"If you lay a hand on this boy," he said calmly, "I'll cut your heart out!"

He may not have meant it, but he said it as if he did; and the lawyer changed his mind about licking me and departed somewhat hastily. Then my defender put up his knife and, turning on me, gave me a lecture on the ethics of good taste in newspaper work. I was in a frame of mind to appreciate what he said, too, for I was scared limber.

That was the summer of the World's Fair. I spent two weeks there. I liked Chicago better than I did the fair, and I spent most of my two weeks rambling about the streets; but, strange to say, I did not hanker for a job on a big-city paper—that was to come later. Nearly everybody in our town went to Chicago that summer, and nearly every adult in the lot wrote at least one letter back to the home paper describing the wonders of the fair. I alone refrained—and I was a writer by profession too! I have been proud ever since of my forbearance and self-restraint.

Two years went by, during which I was steadily doing more and more of the local work on the paper. Some days practically I did it all. The older reporter quit and I formally succeeded to his job on a salary of ten dollars a week. Regularly I wrote four or five columns of stuff a day, and often more. That may sound like a good deal of writing, but plenty of small-town reporters turn out as much copy, day in and day out. It has been my subsequent observation that a small-town reporter is customarily expected to write about four times as much stuff as a big-city reporter, but the big-city man usually writes his about four times as well—bulk against quality.

At the end of the third year a wave of mortality swept the shop. Several of the old-timers died, all in a few months' time.

One of the proprietors died, and the survivor, who was Boss Jim, sold out his interest and retired. His brother quit as editor to go into another line of business, and overnight I was promoted to his place and had my name stuck up at the top of the editorial column as editor. I still did plenty of reporting—all country editors do —but I was the editor just the same, and I was only nineteen years old. I was probably the youngest managing editor of a daily paper in the country; undoubtedly I was the worst. I did not have the judgment or the balance or the experience to fit me for the place; I had only ambition and energy and an ability to throw copy together quickly. And I was as careless and nearly as dangerous as a two-year-old child playing with a box of matches in an oil warehouse.

It was not facts I was after; I only hankered for the details. In a big city I should have been called a faker and yellow. I marvel yet how I got away with it in a small town. But somehow I did! I managed to involve the paper in several good sized libel suits—one of these suits being based not on the story we printed but on the headline I put over it—and I had one or two narrow escapes from being shot by indignant citizens. Down in that country aggrieved persons were not much given to asking damages of a paper that had misrepresented them; they preferred taking it out of the editor's hide. I guess my youth saved me—that and a good stiff bluff on my part. Once or twice I was frightened blue, but I packed a pistol on my hip and talked big and nobody winged me.

It was while I was editor of the paper that I covered my first hanging. And this hanging linked together my first job with my present one, for the victim was a negro who had worked for my father. When I drove that ice wagon he rode on the back end and handled the ice. He was a broad, stocky darky, always polite and respectful in dealing with white people, but a black terror among his own race. Now he was about to be hanged for killing a negro woman and I was to write the story of it for my paper. By our standards it would be about the biggest story we could print, and from my personal standpoint it was invested with a high dramatic quality.

With the editor of the rival paper and two other witnesses I spent the night before the hanging at the jailer's house. We played nickel-limit poker until three o'clock in the morning; then we had a fried-fish breakfast, and about an hour before daylight we went to the jail. The condemned man was already up and dressed in a new suit of black clothes. He wore a stiff white collar and a black tie—probably the first collar and the first tie he had ever worn in his life—and his hands were incased in white cotton gloves, and his brand-new shoes had been given an extra polish by one of the jail trusties. The suit and the shoes were a gift from the sheriff; the white gloves were George's own idea. His name was George, but his own people had a name for him—a tribute to his record. They called him Devil!

This minute I can shut my eyes and see the picture of him as he paced up and down the narrow jail corridor in the half light of the flickery gas-jets. I can see his eight-dollar suit bunching in the back; see his huge gloved hands fluttering like two white pigeons as he chanted snatches of hymns and broken prayers—working himself up to the state of exaltation that sends so many of his race to the gallows shouting-happy. Plastered against the barred cell-doors beyond, like bats, hung ten or a dozen negroes, their eyeballs standing out from the shadowy background like so many pairs of shiny china marbles. In time to the cadences of Devil they crooned and groaned in a wholly sympathetic half-hysterical chorus.

Suddenly the condemned man paused and began a moving exhortation to all sinners within the sound of his voice to take warning before it was too late, and repent of their sins. And those others promised him they would—promised him with sobs and shouts and amens and camp-meeting hallelujahs! He warmed to his theme.

"Dis time to-night I'll be in glory!" he told them, his voice rising in a long swing and then sinking low again. "I'll hab a shimmerin' robe upon me an' golden slippahs on my feet. An' I's comin' back to dis yere sinful world to hant de wicked an' de lost!"

From the cells came a long, shivering groan, and through the bars we could see his scared audience shaking in their terror.

"Yas, suh," he went on, "I's comin' back to dis world to-night. An' dat ain't all—I's comin' back to dis yere jail!"

A howl of piteous entreaty arose, so loud that it reached the ears of the negroes gathering in the gloom outside; and they took it up and the whole air everywhere seemed filled with the sound of their wailings. A voice from one of the cells cut through this:

"Devil," pleaded a little negro prisoner, "please don't do dat! Come back to dis world ef you wants to, but don't come back to dis jail! Ef you does, Devil, I warns you right now I's gwine tear down dis yere w'ite folks' jail gittin' out it."

The time came to read the death warrant—a needless cruelty imposed by the statutes of our state. There was a hitch here. The sheriff had been made ill by the task ahead of him and was violently nause-

ated in the jail office. One of his deputies
was outside testing the rope and the trap.
The other deputy was so nearsighted that
in the bad light he could not make out to
read fine print; but the death warrant must
be read aloud in the presence of the condemned—the law so provided. Somebody
shoved a paper into my hands and I found
myself stumbling through the awesome
document, while Devil stood facing me with
his hands crossed and spread flat upon his
breast. He was drinking in the big, im-
pressive words and glorying—visibly glorying—in the importance of his position. And
when I was through he thanked me.

"Young Cap'n," he said, giving me my
old ice-wagon title, "I always knowed dat
ef ever you could do pore ole George a favor you suttinly would. Thanky, suh.
kindly."

It was after they had tied his hands behind him and had started the march to the
scaffold that, for the first time, he showed
signs of his distress. His scalp suddenly
contorted until a deep V of ridged flesh

appeared between his eyes—it was still there when they cut him down.

Hundreds of negro women outside, seeing his head rise above the high fence, set up a dismal quavering song of lamentation; and, as though in defiance of them, a group of reckless young negroes began singing the Devil Song—one of those weird chants that guitar-picking minstrel bards among the Southern negroes write to commemorate a notable crime or a great tragedy. This one dealt with Devil's life and his crime and his trial; and now there were added verses, made up on the spot, to describe his hanging. Just as the drop fell a negro stretched on the limb of a tree overhanging the inclosure fainted and tumbled off right at our feet. And either the rope was too long—as it so often is—or it stretched under the weight; and poor Devil's feet touched, and he made a long, sickening job of dying.

We assisted in that hanging—another cub-reporter and I. I had already read the death warrant; now both of us served the law and the ends of mercy. We stood together under the gallows. The agonizing figure of the negro swayed and swung within a yard of us. We saw how the tip of one of his toes was poised exactly upon the peak of a big piece of gravel which lifted above the surface of the jail yard. It sustained his weight—that and the rope about his neck. Something must be done and done quickly else the man would choke by degrees of slow torture; he was making hideous muffled sounds in his throat and twitching and jerking through all of his frame. So one of us caught his bound legs at the bend of the knee and raised them clear and the other kicked the jagged pebble away. His feet did not touch after that although, even so, the margin was so narrow that you could not roll a lead-pencil along the earth beneath him without scraping the soles of his shoes.

A city paper would have played up that story; it had in it all the elements to make a great story—the tragic and the serio-comic, the grotesque, the picturesque, abundant gruesomeness, and a grisly, grim humor. A big-city reporter would have reproduced the whole scene—would have written the color into it and the contrasts; but I was no big-city reporter. I had the training of a country office, and my methods of approaching a subject and of treating it were entirely different.

I handled that story as such stories had always been handled in our country—for home consumption. I wrote four columns of commonplace. I slurred over or left out altogether the things that made Devil's hanging one hanging in a thousand; but in detail I described the last breakfast he ate and the costume he wore. I gave the names of all the witnesses. In my best style I reviewed the crime for which he died, putting in just as many adjectives as the narrative would stand without becoming all adjectives; and I finished off with a condensed account of the trial and short sketches of the jailer's life and the sheriff's life, and a final half column under the subheading: Other Hangings in This County.

I've thought a thousand times since what an opportunity I missed then; but perhaps it was just as well that I missed it. Had I handled the tale differently from the way

I did handle it our subscribers probably
would not have cared for it; whereas my
story appeared to give general satisfaction.
A number of people complimented me on it.

Up to this time no longing for the city
had come to me. Even after I lost my
brief job as managing editor—through a
reorganization that brought the old editor
back—and had been reduced to the ranks,
I was satisfied to go on being a small-town
reporter. I first felt the call of the big town
after something had happened that I am
going to describe later. All my life before
that and since then, right on up to the present day, I have been reading fiction stories
of newspaper offices, in which the hero is
invariably a despised cub reporter, who,
unaided, lands the story of the year, thereby
plastering the star reporters over with envy
and the cruel city editor with shame.

I call them fiction stories advisedly, because reporting is a trade that must be
learned—the same as any other trade is
learned; and, no matter how great the natural aptitude of the beginner may be, he
must sharpen his abilities on the rough

whetstone of actual, laborious experience before he is able to cope with older and better-trained men.

In real life I never but once knew it to happen that the green cub reporter beat out the trained veterans against whom he was pitted. What is still stranger, it happened to me! And it was not because of my skill or my native shrewdness either, for I was shy on both those commodities. It happened just because it happened—it was pure chance; raw, crude luck from the beginning to the end.

Stickfuls

GETTING SET IN NEW YORK
CHAPTER TWO

The Second Stick

CHAPTER II

The Second Stick

I WAS nearly twenty-one years old and had served a four-year apprenticeship on the leading home paper before the yearning for the big town began to gnaw at my young vitals. At twenty I was drawing down twelve dollars a week, a topnotch salary for a reporter in our town, and I fancied myself an exceedingly bright and capable young man. To strangers I always spoke of myself as a journalist; I always thought of myself as a journalist—never as a mere newspaper man. I rode free on the street cars and had a season ticket for the theater—there was only one—and carried a pocketful of telegraph franks and railroad annuals. In those halcyon days a cub reporter on a country paper could get more free transportation over trunk lines than a railroad president can get now. Also, I was the resident correspondent for a list of city papers as long as my arm. I used to pick up a tidy bit of money out of my correspondence. Sometimes my weekly space bills equaled my salary.

This was my situation when in Chicago there was committed a murder that startled the whole country. A broken-nosed ruffian named Christopher Merry, who posed by day as a peddler and by night followed his real vocation as a robber, put his faithful wife to death by slow degrees of almost incredible brutality. As I now recall the story, he sewed the body up into a roll of rags and, with two lesser scoundrels to help him, carried it in a wagon to a secluded spot on a lonely road a few miles from Chicago, and buried it there late at night. One of the three talked too much, was arrested and practically confessed. Appreciating the character of the man, the police threw double loops of men round the block and round the house where they knew the murderer and his remaining accomplice had hidden. Cautiously they closed in and broke down the doors of Merry's flat. The rooms were empty.

The crime itself, the midnight burial of the victim and the manner of the escape—most of all the escape—made a tremendously big story from the Chicago standpoint. Naturally the Chicago police department extended itself to find the fugitives. A big reward was offered for Merry; a smaller, yet a good-sized one, for his accomplice.

For one solid month they captured Chris Merry all over this continent. Every time a country constable saw a stranger with a broken nose he locked him up and wired to Chicago that he had the murderer. At first the Chicago police department and the Chicago newspapers sent men in response to each of these messages. Finally they all got tired of answering false alarms and resolved to remain calm until the real Merry had been arrested.

Meanwhile Merry and his partner, whose name was Smith, had been working their way South. They were aiming for New Orleans and then for Cuba, where they expected to join the insurrectos fighting against Spain and lose themselves some-

where in the interior of the island. It was
a pretty good plan and it might have worked
except that, as they were stealing a ride on a
freight train in Indiana, a sudden cold snap
descended upon them and Merry's feet were
so badly frostbitten that for the time being
he became badly crippled. Every step he
took must have been agony to him; but he
kept going. At the beginning of Christmas week he and Smith crossed the Ohio
River into Kentucky. At Louisville they
climbed into a box car billed for Memphis.
Toward dusk a brakeman discovered them
and they were thrown off at a little station
in the western part of Kentucky, called Fredonia.

That same night a tramp of the harmless
variety known as a gay cat crawled into a
toolshed back of an empty section house below Fredonia to stay until morning. There
he found two more wayfarers. They permitted him to share the quarters with them.
They had a bottle of whisky and they shared
that with him too. Pretty soon the evident
leader of the pair—Merry, as it turned out
—rolled over on his side and went to sleep.
His companion and the tramp sat up to fin-

ish the bottle. Liquor loosened the clack of Smith's tongue and he began to boast of his companion.

"You're just a plain bum," he told the listening gay cat, "but we're both bad guys." He had hauled out a big revolver and he flourished it. "The cops are lookin' for us now for a big job we pulled off in Chi." He produced a clipping from a newspaper from his pocket and showed it to the gay cat. The clipping bore reproductions of pen-and-ink pictures of two men. The names had been cut off, but the likenesses were fair and the startled tramp recognized them as pictures of his new acquaintances. He did not say much, but he did a lot of thinking. He craved to quit such dangerous company as soon as he could. Presently he had his chance. The frayed, greasy clipping dropped from Smith's unsteady fingers and he slept too. The scared gay cat waited until Smith began to snore. Then he rose softly and straightway departed from there —but he took that clipping with him.

The next night, which was the night before Christmas, an unfeeling flagman kicked him off a freight into a roaring snowstorm and the town of Mayfield, Kentucky. Half frozen, he hobbled to the nearest house and begged for something to eat. The head of the house gave him a hot supper and let him thaw out by the kitchen fire. The tramp sought to make his gratitude manifest. He hauled out his treasured clipping and showed it to his host and told how and when he got it.

"I'll bet there's a reward out for them men," he said. "One of 'em's feet is froze and he can't travel far. You better see the sheriff or somebody, and then he kin ketch 'em and you'll git part of the money."

Behold how beautifully the thing worked out! The householder's brother-in-law was the town marshal, a man with more than a local reputation as a shrewd detective. Straightway the tramp was taken to the town marshal's house. There he repeated his story and surrendered the clipping, and then he disappeared without even telling his name. Before morning the Mayfield officer was on his way up the line to Fredonia. He had compared the pen-and-ink drawings in the paper with two photographs upon a circular on file in his office, and he knew he was on the track of Merry and Smith and a big cash prize.

He took up the trail at Fredonia, tracing the two southward down the railroad to Kuttawa, a somewhat larger town. There Merry's frost-cracked feet and his endurance had given out together and the pair had secured lodgings—grim joke!—in the house of the Kuttawa town marshal, who took boarders to help out his official income. Already he was on fairly friendly terms with his two transient guests "from up north." When the Mayfield marshal sought his Kuttawa brother privately and told who he was harboring, the Kuttawa marshal almost had a fit. Upon hearing the size of the reward, he promptly revived.

These two country policemen had better luck than the astute Chicago police department had had. They rounded up the dangerous boarders with ease. Afterward Merry, with a pleased grin, told how he detected them watching the front and rear of the house in the dusk, and how, stealing to a window with his revolver, he twice drew a bead upon the fair target of his host's large white slouch hat. He did not in the least mind killing him, he explained, but in his crippled state he could not hope to get away; so what would be the use? He reasoned it all out, and then he surrendered.

The triumphant marshals carried their prisoners up the road a short distance to Princeton, which was a county seat, locked them up in the county jail, and then telegraphed Chicago headquarters that they had Merry and Smith in custody. But Chicago had heard that tale before—many times. It had got to be a joke. Chicago declined to become excited.

That afternoon, though, a special officer of the Illinois Central Railroad chanced to be in Princeton and he went to the jail to see the prisoners. As it happened, he knew Smith by sight, having met him professionally when he, the detective, was a plainclothes man at Chicago headquarters, before he went to work for the railroad. He hurried right out and wired to Chicago that this time it was Merry and Smith, sure enough; but, first, he warned the jailer of the dangerous character of his charges and advised him against allowing any strangers to see the trapped fugitives, knowing they had a wide acquaintance among traveling yeggmen.

It seemed that some of the Chicago papers had already begun to suspect it might indeed be the far-hunted pair that had been nabbed by two country policemen down in a back county of Kentucky. Two of the papers—I forget which two now—had already started their star reporters south before the definite word came; but the *Tribune,* which had taken a leading hand in scoring the police for inefficiency and which, therefore, had a peculiar interest in the story, waited too long. The *Tribune's* staff man failed to board the last train that would land him in Princeton in time to cover the story the following night.

So the *Tribune's* telegraph editor, as I found out later, wired every one of the *Tribune's* country correspondents within a radius of a hundred miles of Princeton to go there forthwith. He was hoping that out of the crowd of them there might be one who would know enough to handle the story in some sort of fashion. One of these orders came to me and, as it turned out, I was the only country correspondent of the whole lot who obeyed. I went.

Princeton was considerably less than a hundred miles from my town, and within an hour after the telegram reached me I was on my way. It was the first time a job of such size had been intrusted to me and I was swollen with a sense of my importance. At the same time I had only the vaguest idea of how to set about getting my story, or writing it after I got it. When I dropped off the train at Princeton the depot platform was overflowing with townspeople, and at least half of them followed me up the street leading from the station. I felt flattered until one man asked who I was and I told him. Then my escort began to dwindle away. I was lean and tall and I wore a large ulster and a broad-brimmed hat; they had taken me for a Chicago detective who had been expected on that train.

Not knowing exactly what I was to do, except that I was to get an interview with the prisoners—my telegraphed instructions had been most explicit on that point—I marched into the local hotel and registered —the official loafers were pawing over the book to find out my name before I laid the pen down—and then I started for the jail. A volunteer committee went along to show me the way. The jail was a small mildewed-looking brick structure. Viewed from the exterior the most interesting object in connection with it was a gentleman of a stern aspect sitting on the front steps nursing a rifle upon his knees. Across the way two well-dressed young men were pacing up and down, swearing in a feverish and impotent way. Passing them, I gathered from certain remarks of theirs that their preconceived notions of Southern hospitality had suffered a severe jolt.

I crossed over to the jail, my heart beating a little faster than usual, showed my credentials to the person with the rifle, stated my business and said that I desired to be admitted to the presence of Merry

and Smith. He was courteous enough—
but he did not let me in. As I now recollect,
he said the Twelve Apostles themselves
could not get into that jail except over his
dead body. It seemed that the jailer was a
literal person. He had been warned against
letting any strangers see his principal prisoners, and he was not letting any strangers
see them. It made no difference who they
were or where they came from; if they were
strangers that was amply sufficient for him.
I began to understand why the two well-
dressed young men across the street had
shown so much heat. They were Chicago
reporters—but also they were strangers.

I stood there a bit, wondering what I
would do next. Then I remembered that
I knew the mayor of the town. He was a
friend of my father's—they had been soldiers in the same regiment during the Civil
War. I asked the way to his house. He was
at home. He listened to me and then locked
his arm in mine and led me back to the jail
—past those two fuming Chicago reporters,
past the deputy on guard at the door and
into the jailer's office. The jailer was a

grizzled old chap with a game leg. The mayor introduced me to him.

"Jim," he said, "this boy is Josh Cobb's son and Bob Cobb's nephew."

If I had been his own long lost son that jailer could not have been any gladder to see me. He had been a gunner in a Confederate battery commanded by my uncle. When the mayor explained that I represented a city paper and wanted to see his two charges, Jim reached for his keys.

"That there Chicago officer told me not to admit any strangers," he said, "and I ain't aiming to do so; but, son, you're no stranger—you're just the same as home-folks."

He led the way into the body of the jail. It was a little, smelly, dark, unventilated cubbyhole of a place, with blank brick walls on two sides and rows of cells on the other two, and a red-hot stove in the middle. Half a dozen ragged negroes—the ordinary occupants of the establishment—were squatted round the stove. My men were in the largest of the cells. The jailer was not taking any chances with them. There was an

extra heavy lock on the door of their cage,
and for precaution he had put heavy leg
irons on them and made their chains fast to
the bars.

The jig was up with them and they knew
it. Besides, they had the pride of criminals
who had outwitted their natural enemies,
the police, and they were ready and willing
to talk about their achievement. Considerably embarrassed, I told them I was serving the Chicago *Tribune* and wanted to get
a statement from them; then I stopped, not
knowing what to do or say next. They did
the rest themselves. They guyed my embarrassment and made fun of my broad-
brimmed hat and my budding mustache, but
they talked. How they did talk! There
was no mention made of the murder—by
unspoken consent all three of us avoided
that painful subject—but they told me how
they had watched the loops of policemen
closing in on them and how they had
broken through the twin cordons. They
gave me a circumstantial account of their
subsequent wanderings, with the dates and
names of the different towns they had vis-

ited; and I put it all down just as they told
it to me. If I hesitated over the spelling of
a proper name one or the other would help
me out; and at the end Merry himself took
my notebook through the bars and, holding
it upon his knee, drew in it a rough dia-
gram of the Chicago streets through which
they had fled, indicating the location of his
flat and the lines of the police. He made a
couple of dots to show where two detectives had been standing when he and Smith
slipped by, not six feet away, and he wrote
down the names of these two detectives. He
marked the place where they had scaled the
structure of an elevated road and so had
walked away to safety right above the heads
of a dozen watchful officers. For Chicago
purposes the stuff he was giving me was
worth its weight in gold almost—only I did
not know it.

At the end of half an hour they sent me
away with a farewell gibe or two. I got out.
The old jailer wanted me to go home with
him for supper; but I declined because in a
dim sort of way I was beginning to realize
I had the making of a pretty good yarn con-

cealed about me, and I burned to get it under way. Going back to the hotel, I ran into the two town marshals who had made the arrests, and they supplied me with full details of their part of the story. One of them, the Mayfield marshal, furnished a graphic enough word picture of the vanished tramp who had given the first clue.

The Western Union Company had its office in the lobby of the hotel, and when I got back there the two Chicago men were sitting alongside the operator, who was a young nervous-looking fellow, hardly more than a boy in age. They were turning out copy, seemingly by the ream, while an admiring audience of citizens looked on over their shoulders. To this day I do not know whether they ever saw the two prisoners, but if they did I doubt whether they got so much copy out of the pair as I did. I still believe that blood-dyed villain of a Merry actually took pity on my greenness and gave me a better story than perhaps he would have yielded up to a skilled reporter. Probably I was the only person on earth who felt sorry when they hanged him a few months later in the Cook County Jail.

Anyway, there sat the Chicago men writing away like mad, with the lone operator looking decidedly uneasy and fidgety as he saw how fast the scribbled sheets accumulated in front of each of them. Abashed by the presence of these luminaries from the big city, I timidly introduced myself and announced that I was on hand to serve the *Tribune*. One of them, the younger of the two, merely looked at me with raised eyebrows and a grin on his face and went on writing. The other man was kinder. He stopped long enough to tell me something of the records of Merry and Smith, and out of the clutter in his overcoat pocket he dug up for me a clipped-out Sunday special, which reviewed the killing of the woman and the police end of the escape. This clipping helped me mightily later on; but when I inquired regarding the chances of putting some copy on the wire they both agreed promptly that they expected to keep the operator busy until midnight or later. Neither one of them seemed to think it worth his while to ask whether I had seen

Merry and Smith; if they had I should
undoubtedly have turned over to them the
whole of my story. But they did not ask,
and I did not tell them.

I went in to supper, and over the fleet
of white-china canary-bird bathtubs containing the meal I read and digested the
clipping that had been given me. After
supper I headed for the depot to make my
arrangements for filing with the Postal.
The Postal man, as I knew, acted as train
dispatcher for the railroad, and because the
Tribune's instructions to me had come over
the Western Union I should have preferred
to use the Western Union; but I knew it
was the Postal or nothing. As I was starting I met a man I knew—the circulation
manager of a Louisville newspaper. He
had been a reporter before he went into the
business office. He had an evening off, and
through sheer love of the game—and possibly also through pity for my evident inex-
perience—he offered to go along with me
and help me put my story together.

At the station the night operator made
us welcome in his little crowded office, but

he said he was going to be so busy clearing trains that it would be nine o'clock for sure, and maybe ten, before he could touch anything else. However, he found time to flash the *Tribune* a synopsis of my story— I did have sense enough to write that—and right away the answer came back. It ran something after this fashion:

Sounds like a big story. Write it fully. Lead off with story of the flight and the route followed by fugitives, so we can prepare maps and diagrams from your telegraphed descriptions. Then send everything in detail.

My enthusiasm grew; I realized now that I really did have a tale worth telling. I started off with a flamboyant and be-adjectived introduction of half a column or more, and then I settled down to spin out my yarn. Long before the operator was ready for me I was frightened at the mass of copy I had produced. Never before had I done a special of more than five or six hundred words, and here already were two or three thousand words at least—and just getting well started! Could any paper on earth print such a staggeringly big, long dispatch? Would any paper pay the tolls on it? Sup-

pose the *Tribune* changed its mind and refused to take it! Inwardly I was a scared
young person, but I kept right on writing
just the same; and all this time, at five and
ten minute intervals, the impatient telegraph editor in Chicago kept flashing in-
quiries, wanting to know why in Halifax
and other localities that story did not
come on.

Finally, along toward half past nine, the
operator got his tracks and his wires cleared
of railroad business and was ready to tackle
my manuscript. He was a dandy operator
too; he fairly made that key of his beg for
mercy. It was he who suggested that I
break my story up into sections, with a separate dateline and separate lead for each in-
stallment of it—which was a good idea, because it gave my volunteer assistant, the circulation manager, a chance to write something. He proceeded to write in detail what
I had already written in bulletin form—the
narrative of the escape and the flight—
while I, now altogether reckless of consequences and filled with the unapproachable
joy of creation and authorship, turned my-

self loose on what I conceived to be a thrilling picture of that pair of trapped ruffians, sitting with their chained ankles in that little box of a jail, bragging how they had outwitted the whole Chicago police department. I always liked to do descriptive stuff, anyhow, whereas a recital of plain facts hampered my style and circumscribed my fancy. I almost wrote my young head off. Pretty soon the operator had another notion.

"See here, kid," he said; "I'm sending over a loop directly into the *Tribune* shop; but if I had another man here to help me out he could send into the city office of the Postal and they could nustle the stuff round by messenger and save a lot of time. My day relief lives up the street a piece, near the hotel. Why don't you go up there and roust him out? He'll be glad to come down here and help out with all this jag of stuff that you two are piling up."

I put on my hat and coat and went. It was nearly eleven o'clock then, and it was snowing a little and the road under my feet was as black as ink. I stumbled along feeling my way until I came to the hotel, and I went in to ask the clerk the exact location of the house of the man I was looking for to help me out.

The clerk had just started to tell me when he broke off and pointed over my shoulder and said: "Why, there he comes now!"

The young Western Union operator had played out. Unused as he was to handling big newspaper jobs, his fingers had cramped. It was only a question of a little while until he would have to give up altogether. In this emergency he had suggested that maybe the Postal's day man, as an act of neighborly accommodation, might be willing to help him; and so one of the two Chicago reporters had gone to the Postal operator's house and waked him up and was now bringing him in. His face was puckered with sleepiness and he had an overcoat on over his nightshirt. Yawning and stretching himself, he was just sitting down at an instrument when I reached his side and told him I wanted his services too.

Still half asleep he started to explain the situation while the two Chicago men glowered angrily at me and probably cursed me inwardly for a meddlesome young cub.

"I've promised to help these gentlemen out," he said. "They're in a fix, so they tell me."

I had a flash of sagacity—the only real flash I produced unaided during the whole night.

"Yes," I said; "but this is the Western Union you're working for—isn't it? You're working for them for nothing, but I've got a slew of stuff to go over your own line—the Postal."

"In that case," he said, "it's a different thing."

Those two Chicago men each with a great wad of copy yet to be sent, protested and begged and swore; but he Postal man went with me. He was no slouch of an operator either. In five minutes after we two reached the depot my story—or rather our story, for the circulation man from Louisville did his share—was feeding into the *Tribune's* telegraph room over two wires at once. Pretty soon one of the telegra-

phers broke off long enough to take a line
for me and toss it over:

Let it all come.   Spread yourself and keep sending
until we say stop.

I spread myself all right. I wrote and
wrote and wrote! I elaborated my description of the jail scene. I piled the local
color on by the hodload. I described the
principal local characters in the story—the
jailer, his vigilant deputy, the two town
marshals, the unnamed tramp who had
sicked them on to their quarry. I humped
my shoulders and curled my legs round the
legs of my chair, and the sheets of copy slid
out from under my fingers in a white
stream.

At intervals one of the Chicago men
would come in and want to know when a
wire would be clear; and I, remembering
that mossy and venerable yarn so dear to
the heart of every green reporter—the one
about the war correspondent who sent the
Book of Genesis by cable in order to hold
the wire against all opposition until his
paper went to press carrying the exclusive

account of a great battle—I, remembering that tale, would say to him that I could not tell him when I should be through or anyway near through, and then I would go on writing. He would curse and groan and go out and slam the door with unnecessary violence and I could hear him tramping up and down the platform. The operator of the Western Union had petered out altogether along about midnight; I found that out later.

I held my wires—both of them. I wrote everything I could think of and then wrote it over again. I wrote until my fingers were black from repeated sharpenings of my pencil—wrote until my right hand was numb up to the wrist. My head swam and my eyes blurred, but I kept on writing; and the wonder of it was the *Tribune* kept on taking what I wrote. I imagine one of my operators appreciating the joke of it, must have quietly told the operator at the other end what the situation was; and possibly the *Tribune* people approved the notion of my holding the lines and shutting out my rivals. Anyhow they let me go ahead. It

was nearly two o'clock in the morning—
Sunday morning—before they finally shut
off my flow of literature. The message
read:

That's enough. Good stuff! Good boy! Good
night!

I got up on my feet, stiff and staggering
and grimed to the eyebrows with graphite
dust; and just then I heard the whistle of
the train that would take me back home. I
told my friend, the circulation man, I would
send him a fair share of what the *Tribune*
sent me. Then I climbed wearily aboard
the train and curled up in a seat in the day
coach; and the next thing I knew the con-
ductor was literally dumping me in a coma-
tose heap off upon the platform at my station. I managed to get home and to bed,
and there I stayed until dusk that evening.
Then I got up and dressed, and went down
to the book store and waited until the Chicago Sunday papers came in. I bought a
copy of the *Tribune*. I took one look at the
paper and my eyes popped with amazement
and pride—but mostly with pride.

The last column of the first page—under flaring headlines—was mine! Nearly five columns of the second page were mine! I had written the best part of a page for the Chicago *Tribune*. True, the copy readers had pruned a lot of the foliage off my introductions, and they had chopped out a good many of my most cherished adjectives; but in all essentials it was my story and, what was more, a good share of it was exclusive, as I found by comparison of the *Tribune* with the other Chicago papers. To be sure, I was not responsible really for this exclusiveness. Most of it had been forced upon me, so to speak; and, anyway, I did not value that part of it as an older and wiser newspaper man would have valued it. What mainly concerned me was the length of the story, as measured in columns. I spent a happy evening picking out my brain children that were studded thick through the yarn.

On Monday morning I got a letter postmarked Chicago, and I opened the envelope to find inside a single sheet of notepaper bearing the heading: Editorial Rooms, the

Tribune. The following lines were written on it in a somewhat crabbed hand:

Dear Sir: You did excellent work in covering the Merry story for this paper, and I wish to thank you.

I have instructed the cashier to send you a check for fifty dollars as a bonus.

Yours truly,

JOSEPH MEDILL.

I was tickled naturally to get such a letter—particularly was I tickled by the second paragraph—but in the abysmal depths of my fathomless ignorance I attached no particular importance to the fact that Joseph Medill himself had written, with his own hand, to express his appreciation of what a stranger had done for his paper. I knew that the editor or the publisher of the *Tribune* was a man named Medill, but in my conceived estimates the only really great and conspicuous editors of America were Henry Watterson, Henry W. Grady and Murat Halstead, in the order named. A Medill more or less meant nothing to me. I carried that letter about in my pocket for a day or two, and then I tore it up or lost it or something. I wish I had it now.

Anyway, when my check came from the *Tribune* at the end of the month I forgot all about the letter; for the fifty dollars was what Mr. Medill had said it would be —a bonus—and in addition to the fifty they had allowed my expense account and given me full space rates for the story. In all it came to something like one hundred dollars. Here in one magnificent lump was as much as I made in salary in two months. It was the largest amount I had ever owned at one time in my life. It was hard to believe. If a man working one night could make that much off of a city paper how much could he make in a month or in a year? The possibility staggered the imagination; at least it staggered my imagination. From that hour dated my desire to work on a big newspaper—a Chicago or New York newspaper; but it was to be several years before my wish came true.

I was sixteen years old when I broke into the newspaper business. At twenty-six I had broadened considerably. Once or twice I had also been flattened pretty severely, and there were a few permanent dents in my bump of assurance. Also I was beginning to get cured of the adolescent belief that the only good writing was this so-called fine writing, full of adjectives and screaming metaphors and reverberating periods. In other words, I had quit writing at the top of my voice all the time; and when a young reporter—or an old one—learns that great and difficult lesson there is hope for him ultimately, I reckon.

Meanwhile I had one illuminating and disillusionizing experience with city news-paper work. Through my work as a correspondent I got a trial job on a paper printed in a city of a quarter of a million population or so, in a state to the north of us. I was twenty-three then and full of pleasing delusions about myself. As for the paper, it was one of a string of afternoon papers published under the same owner-ship and the same general management in the Middle West and Southwest. Green as a young gourd, I reported for duty one October morning at seven-thirty and was set to work in the telegraph room. The telegraph room was intolerably dirty and intolerably crowded—filled to the ledges of its smeared windows with telegraph operators, telegraph editors in an advanced state of distraction, tobacco smoke, coal soot, the click of Morse instruments, the clatter of typewriters and loud cries.

This newspaper was run on weird lines. Even I—raw as I was—could tell that. Its policy was to print everything that happened anywhere, whether it was of interest to anybody or not; and as space in its pages was limited, owing to the use of big headlines and copious illustrations, there was a large staff constantly engaged for eight or nine or ten hours a day in reducing big stories to small ones and smaller ones to countless hundreds of three and four line paragraphs. Enough energy was wasted in that shop, it seemed to me, to get out three or four papers. Moreover the whole establishment spent most of its time standing on its head and whirling round.

Every hour nearly, somebody was being promoted or reduced or disciplined or rewarded or hired or fired and then hired back again. Hysteria passed for enthusi-

asm and mania for efficiency. All hands
worked at a high tension, without apparently getting anywhere. Yet, strange to say,
that paper made plenty of money, and from
the system of which it was a part a lot of
good newspaper men have been produced.
I take it as the strongest evidence of their
native talents that they could serve for any
length of time in such an atmosphere and
still be good newspaper men.

In my first city job I lasted four fevered,
nightmarish weeks; and in those four weeks
we shifted managing editors twice. One
of them had a craving for signed statements,
so in each edition we printed a collection of
signed statements from all sorts of people
on all sorts of subjects. His successor believed fervently in extras. He measured
enterprise by the number of extras he could
run off in a single day. He got out extras
on the slightest provocation and on no
provocation at all; and in the fleeting intervals between extras he flew round, popeyed and wild-haired, yelling conflicting
orders at nobody in particular. He always

yelled. I bet when he talked in his sleep he yelled.

As I said, I lasted four weeks. Toward the end of my fourth week, on a Friday, I was told that my salary was to be raised three dollars a week; but at the end of that week, on a Saturday, without any warning at all I was discharged. It appeared that there was an elderly gentleman at a central point who had supervision of all the papers on the circuit; and when the gross receipts of any one paper for a given week fell off, or when the payroll ran up, or his liver troubled him, or the morning was rainy, or the breakfast eggs didn't taste right, it was his pleasing custom to order a wholesale staff reduction by telegraph. I was the sufferer by one of these blighting devastations. About eight or ten others were let out at the same time. They came from all the departments of the paper— the business office, the circulation room, the city room and the telegraph room. Later I found out that in the telegraph room the choice of a victim lay between me and another young fellow who had joined the force a day or two before I came on. He had a wife and I had none, and, anyway, he knew infinitely more about city newspaper work than I did; so he stayed. He stuck to the ship through any number of subsequent cyclones and simoons and eventually rose to be one of the leading men in the organization, and became one of the most capable managing editors in this country.

So I got my plank-walking papers. In letting me out, the man in charge did not show any great degree of finesse. He simply told me he did not want me any longer. I got even though. The upheaval that had put him on top was followed by one that put him on the bottom, and made him a plain reporter for the same sheet of which he had been editor—such was their pleasing custom in that shop—and months later he was sent down into our state to cover a big murder story, and I had the supreme joy of beating him on a couple of its important developments.

That was to come later though. Here it was less than a month since I had left home with a flourish of trumpets—"to accept an important and lucrative position with the metropolitan press" was the way the home paper put it—and now I was going back after having been bodily fired; my old job was gone and no new one in sight. I had been in town only a couple of days and was still coining excuses to account for my unexpected return, when I got a telegram offering me a place on the city staff of the same paper that had just let me out of its telegraph room. But my wounds were still bleeding; I did not even answer the message. In the frame of mind I was in then I would not have done another lick of work for that paper if they had given me the whole shop. Besides, I thought I was about to connect with the leading afternoon paper of the biggest town in my state of Kentucky.

I did connect with it and I stayed there three years—three reasonably happy, busy years. During this period I got married. When we stood up before the minister and I repeated after him the words, "with all my worldly goods I thee endow," I could not help grinning inwardly. All my worldly goods, as nearly as I could recall at the moment, consisted of two suits of clothes, a set of Ridpath's History of the World, and a collection of postage stamps. My salary was eighteen dollars a week.

The end of my third year in the metropolis of the state found me acting as staff correspondent, and covering all the big political stories that broke loose in the state—they broke frequently in that state, where politics was and still is the main diversion of the male populace—and between times I was doing a column of jingles and supposedly humorous paragraphs.

There was a period, though, of many months on end when there was mighty little time for running a humorous column —I was too busy following the political fortunes and the last days on earth of State Senator William Goebel to be working on any sidelines. Here was a man who should have a book all to himself; it would have to be a big book, too, fitly to cover the subject. Since he passed, I have met a good many of the distinguished men of this country, but I have yet to meet one who impressed me as being mentally superior to

William Goebel, that son of a Pennsylvania
German, whose ambitions and whose death
—and the manner of it—practically plunged
Kentucky into civil war. He was a Na-
poleon of politics if ever one lived. He had
audacity, ruthlessness, a genius of leader-
ship, an instinct for absolute despotism, a
gift for organization, a perfect disregard
for other men's rights or lives where his own
wishes were concerned; the brain to plan
and the will to execute. He had devoted
followers by the thousand, and hundreds
called him their friend, but I do not believe
any living creature ever read the inside of
that dark and lonely soul of his. Had he
lived, I am firmly convinced he either would
have ruled the Democratic party in the na-
tion or he would have wrecked it. He loved
power as drunkards love their bottle and he
would have waded through blood up to his
armpits to have his way. One man—Colonel
John Sanford—stood in his path and Goebel
shot him to death in the streets of Coving-
ton. Sanford tried to draw, but Goebel
beat him to it. Even so, there is no doubt
but that Goebel aimed at the ultimate bet-

terment of plain people; the trouble was that his good motives were tinctured by the lust for authority which gnawed at the man day and night, making him a malignant and a dangerous force. In Southern public life he loomed as a curious and an alien pinnacle.

By a great many of the members of the old political oligarchy of the state—which finally he overthrew—he was called an intruder and an interloper and a presumptuous, ill-mannered upstart. They dubbed him poor white trash. They hated him piously. They had reason to—he brought their century-old political aristocracy smashing down in ruins about their heads and did it, too, while defying all traditions of office-seeking and office-holding which the fathers of the faith had built up. He had none of the hand-shaking, pat-'em-on-the-back tricks of the typical Kentucky job-hunter. He belonged to no old family. He was no orator—another point of difference between him and the run of our reigning political class. He had no social graces. In mixed company he was embarrassed and showed it. He was cold and secluded, an aloof figure and a malformed one, a machine politician with a machine-made personality. He had lieutenants to do his bidding. But in Goebel's camp there was only one commander—and that was Goebel.

When I first knew him he was a state senator and a candidate for the Democratic nomination for governor. By trick and device, by main strength and brutal force, he wrested the nomination from a hostile convention and split the party wide open. At the election, on the face of the returns, he was defeated by a Republican whose candidacy had been backed by a great number of disgruntled Democrats. He contested the result before the General Assembly and was about to be seated when an assassin shot him down from a window of the Executive building on the old State House Square at Frankfort. He lingered five days—long enough to take the oath of officer as governor—and then dying, left as a malign legacy to his state the active seeds of a political feud which after the lapse of more than twenty years have not quit sprouting.

I followed Senator Goebel through his campaigning before the nomination and after it. I sat at one of the press-stands on the stage of Music Hall in Louisville where the convention was held, and from that vantage point, not once but half a dozen times, I saw guns drawn and ducked under my table to be out of the road of the bullets. I heard the shot that felled him on a cold January morning of 1900 and, hearing it, I ran out of the Legislative Hall and was one of those who helped to carry the stricken man away. I did not send the first bulletin of the assassination but I think I did send the first coherent story of it. From the men who had been with him when he dropped I got the hurried details while we were bearing him those three blocks through the street to the old Capitol Hotel, and rushed them over the wire to my paper. I covered the captures, under exciting circumstances, of several of the men accused of confederating to murder Goebel, and I covered the first trials of three of these alleged conspirators—Caleb Powers, Henry Youtsey and James Howard. First and last, I worked on one phase or another of the Goebel story for upwards of a year. It was hard work but it was great training for a young reporter and there was never a dull hour in it.

There were many distinctly thrilling moments in it. Some three months after Goebel was shot a group of us one afternoon were sitting in front of the telegraph office discussing—as usual—the crime in one or another of its phases. A member of the Frankfort police force, a fat good-natured man named Wingate, joined us. The talk eddied back to the day of the assassination. Each of us told what he did that crowded morning. My turn presently came. I said:

"I was in the wash room on the first floor back of the library. I had just taken my coat off and rolled up my sleeves preparatory to washing my hands when I heard the shots. To me they sounded as though they had been fired between the Legislative Hall and the Executive Building. Bareheaded and leaving my coat behind I ran out of the side door to see what had happened. Three men had picked up Goebel and were hurrying with him toward the main gate. I remembered where there was a picket out of the fence about half way up the block toward the corner of the Square. So I took a cross cut. I ran diagonally across the lawn, passing just under the windows of the Executive Building, and squeezed through that gap in the panel and was out in the street just as the men with Goebel in their arms reached that point. That was where I joined them and———"

"Say," broke in Policeman Wingate— "Say listen: Now I know who the fellow was I come so blamed near takin' a few wing-shots at. Me, I came out of the front door less than half a minute after the shootin'. I knew already who it was that was shot—a fellow had just bumped into me, yellin' that Goebel had been murdered. So I pulled my gun and jumped for the open. As I came out on the porch the first thing I saw was a long-legged fellow, in his shirt sleeves, and no hat on, with his hair

flying out behind him, tearin' across the
yard. It looked to me like he was trying
to get away from there as quick as he could.
I said to myself, 'That must be the fellow
that did the shootin'.' So I drew a bead on
him. Somebody ran against me by accident
and knocked up my arm. I pulled down
again and was just about to let go when a
Representative grabbed holt of me and said,
'Hold on, don't shoot. I know that man.'
Before I could ask him who the man was
he'd darted away and then when I looked
again I couldn't see the bare-headed fellow
any more. And now by gum I find out it
was you I came so near pluggin' away at.
All this time I've been wonderin' in my own
mind who the devil that long-legged man
was? Say, boy, I'm right glad I didn't
shoot you that day."

I was right glad, too.

Now I got an offer to go back to the town
where I was born and take the editorial
management of a new paper that had just
been started there. From a newspaper
standpoint things had changed in the old
town. The paper upon which I served

my apprenticeship had changed hands so often that people almost forgot the newest owner's name. It had lost a good deal of its prestige and most of the characteristics that had made it so distinctive in the earlier days, and its circulation stood still while the town grew. The new paper had a successful publisher from upstate behind it, and it was making a hard fight for influence and business; it was getting them too. It had a modern plant—linotype machines, a perfecting press, a stereotyping outfit and a membership in the Associated Press. It had even a small art department. This was the shop from which I now accepted a call, as clergymen say.

I guess no man ever worked harder than I did during the next two and a half years. Being the editor meant that I not only handled all the copy that went into the paper, but wrote a good share of it myself. I read most of the proof—all of it sometimes—wrote the heads, dug up Sunday features—and wrote most of them—read all the exchanges and made up the paper. We printed eight papers a week—a regular

number every afternoon, an ambitious
Sunday-morning issue, and a weekly edition. As our owner did not believe in holi-
days, we printed even on Christmas Day
and the Fourth of July.

There were internal complications to
add to my other cares. We had trouble
with our press, with our composition, with
our stereotyping. We had trouble finding
and holding a staff for the editorial room—
most of the time my staff consisted of one
male reporter, one woman reporter, and a
boy just out of high school. It seemed to
me that day or night I never quit working.
In the afternoon, as soon as we had got out
the daily, I would start right in again, providing time copy for the night shift on the
linotypes—we ran the machines pretty
much all the time to get the worth of the
money out of them. Our Sunday edition
was a hungry, yawning thing that ate up
reams of copy. I prided myself on filling
it with strictly home-brewed specials instead of using reprint or syndicate articles
—and that was no easy job, either, let me
tell you! I ate many of my meals on my

desk, a fork in one hand and a pencil in the other, doing snatches of work between bites and taking bites between snatches of work. Many and many a time I have gone to work at seven-thirty o'clock Saturday morning and worked right on through with scarcely a break until three or four or even five o'clock Sunday morning; then put the Sunday issue to press and staggered home, a total wreck, to sleep like a log until noon. But by the middle of Sunday afternoon I would be digging through a mountain of exchanges, trying to find enough reprint to keep the night shift happy until Monday, when the week's grind would start all over again.

It was drudgery—manual and mental labor of the most exacting sort—but I was proud of my job and proud of the paper we turned out. I was fairly young to be in sole editorial management of a paper of such pretensions, and I was drawing a bigger salary—so my employer used to remind me at frequent intervals—than any so-called country editor in the state. I was getting thirty dollars a week. But the strain began to tell on me. There had been a time when I didn't have a nerve in my body. I might get dog-tired, but my nerves never misbehaved. Now I began to develop a chronic grouch. I was peevish and fussy and I worried over small things. I had dizzy spells in the office too. Once I almost fainted across my desk. All work and no play was making Jack a dull boy.

All this time I had been secretly nursing my longing to try the big city, and as these warning signs of a coming nervous breakdown multiplied I thought about that and dreamed about it more and more. I felt pretty sure of getting a job in Chicago any time I wanted it, but across a thousand intervening miles the lure of New York, which comes to every newspaper man at least once in his life, was stretching out to me and tightening its grip on me every day. In New York, so I had heard, newspaper men were paid salaries which, measured by the only standards I knew, seemed fabulous. Several men who had worked with me had gone to New York and had made good there. Stories of their success filtered back and filled me with envy. One, I heard, was earning regularly sixty-five dollars a week—it sounded like a fortune. Yet, when we were working together as reporters, I had topped him by three dollars a week. If he had got along so well why could I not get along too? Then there was the glamour of New York itself. I had read those fiction stories of the wild Bohemian life that newspaper men in New York led, and of their thrilling adventures.

I mulled over it for months. I reckon I changed my mind as often as twice or three times a day. It took a lot of studying and some courage to reach a decision in favor of a change. You see I had a family dependent on me; I was drawing a big salary, for our town; I occupied a position of prominence in the community—all those things counted—and I had a job that would last as long as I lasted. The certainty in my own mind that I couldn't last much longer was what finally drove me to jump. Even then it was my wife who pushed me over the edge. She had ten times my nerve.

When, finally, I got my own consent to

take the plunge I went the full limit. I burned my bridges behind me. I surrendered my job unconditionally; I shipped my wife and child—I had a little girl a year old—to my father-in-law's, and from my father-in-law I borrowed two hundred dollars. One blazing-hot August day I climbed aboard a train and started for New York. My brain was whirling hotly, but my feet were ice-cold; part of me was scared limp and the rest of me was full of glad visions.

I did not know that midsummer was the worst possible time of the year to be looking for a newspaper job in New York. I did not know that in summer most of the papers were laying off men instead of hiring them. I did not know much of anything about New York except that I was going there to break in.

Stickfuls

GETTING SET IN NEW YORK
CHAPTER THREE

The Third Stick

CHAPTER III

The Third Stick

WITH something less than two hundred dollars in my pocket and an imposing sheaf of letters of introduction in the top tray of my trunk I reached New York at nine o'clock on a spitting-hot August night. As the ferryboat waddled out like a fat duck from its nest in the Jersey City slip I stood at her bow and had my first view of the Big Town. There weren't as many skyscrapers then as there are now, but there were enough.

It was the greatest sight I had ever seen, the most inspiring, the most exhilarating—and the most daunting. It stirred me clear up to the roots of my back hair, and it scared me clean down to the nails of my toes. This was the oyster I had come to open and find the meat inside—and maybe, if I had luck, a pearl or two. All of a sudden I realized what a whale of an oyster it was!

If my legs had been cut off at the ankle at
that minute I reckon I shouldn't have bled
a drop; but if I had cold feet in the most
aggravated form I likewise had the courage of desperation that keeps a forlorn hope
from being too forlorn. I had burned the
woods behind me. I just had to make good
—that was all.

That was a good many years ago; but to
this good day I never cross the Hudson
River and see the man-made mountain
ranges of Manhattan blocked out against
the eastern sky that I do not have again, in
some degree, the feelings I had that night;
and I say to myself that I know better than
most native-born the sensations that come
to the alien when he stands on the steerage
deck among his fellow immigrants and see˜
dead ahead the new world rising out of the
water—because, to all intents and purposes,
I was an alien then, too, and was coming to
a brand-new world myself.

I had the address of a boarding house in
West Fifty-seventh Street; but, being uncertain of my ability to find my way about
the streets at night, I registered overnight

at a hotel that had been recommended to me
as one much patronized by Southerners.
Issuing forth from the café after a late
supper, I looked round the lobby for some
fellow Southerner to talk to, having already developed an ache of profound lone-
liness. There was just one person in sight
who seemed to wear the earmarks—a
middle-aged gentleman, with the white
mustache and the long white goatee of the
Confederate colonel of a war drama. He
also wore the regulation black slouch hat.
I sidled over to where he was sitting, took
the chair next to him and presently was
making conversational overtures. He was
willing enough to talk to me, but he was no
Southerner. He was a horsebreeder from
some town in the northern part of Michi-
gan. New York had handed me my first
disillusionment. I went to bed.

But I didn't sleep much. The roar of the
L trains, whizzing by a block away, like
tamed and harnessed meteors; the city
sounds rising from the street, and the new-
ness and uncertainty of my position, all
kept me awake. I was up and dressed in

the morning almost before the milkman got
round; and as I came out into Broadway
and, on a venture, faced south, I saw, half
a mile away, the Flatiron Building, scoured
and bleached in the young sunlight. The
Flatiron Building was new enough then to
be a novelty—there was only one of it. I
had seen a hundred pictures of it. Now I
was seeing the thing itself. Somehow,
looming there in all its hatchet-faced, slice-
of-pie-shaped boldness, it typified New
York for me—its vastness; its power and
bulk; its stone-fronted, steel-cased indiffer-
ence. In a lesser degree it impressed me
much as the ferry ride had done.

There was one man upon whom I was
depending for help to land a job. He
hailed from the town where I was born, and
he had made a success as a newspaper man
in St. Louis and Chicago before he came
East. With a fine large optimism and gen-
erosity he had written me that it would be
no trouble at all, but a pleasure, for him
to find an opening for me in New York. I
called on him the first thing that morning,
to learn the distressing truth that if he

found an opening anywhere he'd want it himself. He had been laid off—so he delicately phrased the state of affairs—and he had had no regular employment for some weeks now; and the silver lining of his change pocket had run low and become exceedingly thin. Five minutes spent in his company, listening to what he had to say, gave me an illuminating insight into the uncertain and transitory character of the average newspaper job in New York— illuminating, but also distressing.

Right away I saw that I could count on no aid from this quarter. I paid my bill at the hotel—the size of it, even for a night's lodging, made me open my provincial eyes —and I escorted my belongings to the boarding house in West Fifty-seventh Street. The next morning I found my way down to Park Row and set about connecting with a job of work. I didn't know that in summer most of the newspapers cut down their staffs and hold them down, letting old men out and not taking any new men on. Perhaps it was just as well I didn't know it.

I started off by spreading my letters of introduction round; all greenhorns in New York do that, I suppose. They didn't get me anywhere; they rarely get any one anywhere, I think. Everybody is willing to write letters of reference and almost nobody is willing to read them—at least, nobody is in New York. I also called on a man whom I had known years before down South. He now had a copy-reading job on a second-rate afternoon sheet; I didn't appreciate at the time, though, that it was a second-rater. I sent my card in to him and he came out and greeted me with studied reserve. As soon as he found out I hadn't come to borrow any money he warmed slightly, but he remained well within the temperate zone throughout the interview. I outlined my situation to him.

"And you gave up a good job as editor of a country paper, where you were you own boss, to come up here and try to break into one of these madhouses!" he exclaimed when I was through. "Old man, you didn't realize when you were well off. Gee! I only wish I had the job you threw up to come here!

"Yes," he said in answer to my next question, "there's a chance you might make good here—if you hang round long enough; but it's a heartbreaking experience, no matter which way the cards fall. You never can tell about this New York newspaper game—not for a minute. These editors are always pretending to look for oranges that haven't been squeezed dry, but mainly they seem to pick lemons. A man who was a wonder in a small town comes on, gets started off wrong or something, and falls down. A man who was a dub out in the country goes right to the top in New York. You never can tell.

"The trouble with all you fellows back home is that you only hear and only want to hear about the few men who succeed in New York. You don't hear about the hundreds of failures.

"Help you land a job? Well now, I tell you, old man, I shouldn't dare try it, even if I thought it would do you any good. I'm holding on to my present job, rotten as it is,

by the skin of my teeth. If I got you a
place and you failed to deliver, the city
editor would probably blame me. He's not
wasting any love on me as it is."

Then he told me to drop in to see him
sometime—vaguely, like that—and excused
himself and went back inside; and I didn't
see him again for two or three years. So
now, after a short period of self-commun-
ion, I realized that I was absolutely on my
own resources—and not any too many of
them; so I set out to worm my way into a
berth unassisted. I spent two solid weeks
canvassing the daily newspapers in New
York. I never got past the anteroom of a
single, solitary one of them. I never saw
anybody above the rank of a head office boy
—but once.

In the forenoons I would make the circuit of the evening papers; in the afternoons I would go to the morning papers.
Sometimes, in answer to the card I sent in,
I would get a scrawled line: "No vacancies
on the staff—City Editor." But oftener the
boy would merely come back and tell me:
"Boss says nuttin' doin'!" Within a day or

two the anteroom attendants all got to know me, and they would grin when I appeared. Never afterward did I, in passing through, see that hopeful row of young men from the country sitting in the anteroom of my paper, waiting to see the city editor, without having a flash of sympathy for them; and then generally a more personal and a more selfish thought would come to me, and I would say to myself: "Right now there's some fellow sitting here who'll probably take my job away from me—if he gets a chance."

When I had finished my afternoon rounds I would get a bite to eat in a quick-lunch place, and then I would start out to see New York. I had my own system for doing this, which was a good one, because it had nothing systematic about it. I would climb aboard a surface car—a cross-town car by preference—and ride on it until I reached a district that looked promising. I would drop off and walk in whatever direction my legs took me, and keep on walking until I got tired; then I'd ask a policeman or somebody to guide me back again to

Broadway or Sixth Avenue. Regularly
every evening I lost myself; but it proved
a mighty good thing for me subsequently,
because in that fortnight I saw more of the
town than many a born-and-bred New
Yorker sees in his whole life. I saw the
Bowery, the East Side, Harlem, China-
town, Greenwich Village, Little Italy, the
waterfront, Wall Street, the Syrian Quarter, the Greek Quarter; and, better still, I
saw them all with new eyes and a mind
open to impressions. Between-times I
would buy and read the papers, studying
their styles of make-up and their ways of
handling stories.

A startling thing to me was the flippancy
with which most of them dealt even with
notable people. Where I'd come from, you
didn't get humorous in print at the expense
of persons of standing in the community
unless you craved excitement and felt the
need of a little violent personal exercise.
Here in this town nobody seemed too high
and mighty to be gibed by reporters and
headliners.

However, those two weeks had passed and

my money was running low, even though I
lived frugally. I had blisters on my feet
and I wasn't any nearer to a job than I had
been when I set out. One noontime I was
sitting on a bench in Madison Square, feeling very tired and considerably discouraged.
It didn't add any to my peace of mind to
consider the bleak, hopeless faces of my
neighbors on the near-by benches. Down-
and-out was written on the face and in the
pose of every one of them.

And right there, just at that minute, I had
an idea. It was better than an idea—it was
an inspiration, born of the needs of the
hour. It lifted me off that bench as if I had
been bee-stung. In half an hour I was in
my hall bedroom in West Fifty-seventh
Street composing a form letter. It wasn't
a very long letter, but into it I tried to pile
a heaping measure of the flippant tone that
seemed so popular in the newspapers. I
guyed the recipient, whoever he might be,
and I guyed myself. I said in effect that
here I was, probably the livest reporter and
the best writer and the ablest editor that
had ever come to New York to uplift its

journalism to the highest possible level, and yet nobody had jumped at the unparalleled opportunity of hiring me; that I had come to town to accept an important and highly lucrative position on some leading paper and was waiting for it; that I could do anything on any paper and do it better probably than the person who was now doing it. I said a lot more like that.

I wound it up, as I recall, after this fashion:

"This is positively your last chance. I have grown weary of studying the wall-paper design in your anteroom. A modest appreciation of my own worth forbids me doing business with your head office boy any longer. Unless you grab me right away I will go elsewhere and leave your paper flat on its back right here in the middle of a hard summer, and your whole life hereafter will be one vast surging regret. The line forms on the left; applications considered in the order in which they are received; triflers and professional flirts save stamps. Write, wire or call at the above address."

I judged that the people who read New York papers liked to be shocked, and liked a note of impudence and irreverence in their daily reading. I meant to see if the same treatment would appeal to the men who furnished the public with this daily literary fodder. It did. The scheme worked for me. It may never work for another man, but in my case it certainly worked. But I'm getting ahead of my tale.

When I had my blanket letter drafted to my satisfaction I went to a stationery shop round the corner and bought a supply of the handsomest paper the shop carried. I found a stenographer in the lobby of a hotel near Columbus Circle, and I had her make thirteen separate copies—not carbon copies—of my letter, addressing each one to a different managing editor. Between giggles, she did it. I signed the completed letters, mailed them in a letter box; and that night I went to bed highly satisfied. I had a feeling that my job was on its way. It was.

Right after breakfast the next morning I put on a newly pressed suit—I had two suits—and made for Newspaper Row. On a chance, I walked into the building of one of the more conservative papers—one that had struck me as being the best written and the best edited of the whole lot. The city room of the morning edition was empty, except for the cleaners—none of the staff had arrived yet; so I climbed a winding flight of iron stairs to the floor above, where the evening edition lived, and sent my card in to the managing editor. I had done this twelve or thirteen times already. Only this time the response was different.

A little man with a pair of tired, shrewd eyes, and a sad smile on his lips, came through a doorway. He was holding my card in one hand and in the other one of my letters.

"Are you the same man who wrote this damn fool letter?" he asked. I said I was.

"Well," he said, "I happen to be the acting managing editor here to-day. If you've got half as much ability as you have gall, consider yourself hired."

"All right," I said; "I'm hired."

He looked at me a minute and his smile widened to half a grin. "Come on in," he said, "and we'll talk this thing over." I followed him across the floor of the city room to his desk in a corner, and there we sat down. He listened while I told him of my experience in the newspaper business—that in my home town I had been reporter and editor; that I had done staff work for three years on the biggest paper in my home state.

"You probably don't know it," he said, "but in my opinion you have one distinct advantage in your favor. The average man who gets all his newspaper training in New York starts in one groove and stays there. He's a specialist along one line. But the country raised man has done everything there is to do on a newspaper; and when he learns the ropes here and picks up the New York way of doing things—if he ever does—he's sure to fit in somewhere. Personally I'd rather take on a new man who knows general newspaper work and doesn't know the town, than one who knows the town and nothing about the inside of a newspaper shop. Now, then, we'll talk salary. What salary do you expect?"

"What I can get," I said. He paused a minute.

"In this establishment," he said, "we start beginners—and that means all new and unknown men—at fifteen dollars a week. It's a rule of the office."

Following what I had heard of the big salaries paid to newspaper reporters in New York, this was a hard jolt. To come to New York, I had just given up thirty dollars a week in a town where one dollar went as far as three would go in New York. I guess my looks betrayed my thoughts.

"Understand," he said, "you won't stick at fifteen. If you, with your experience, aren't worth more than fifteen dollars a week very soon you won't be worth that much—and I'll let you out."

"I'll come for fifteen," I said.

"Good!" he snapped. "When can you start?"

"This minute," I announced.

"Better come back to-morrow morning around eight o'clock," he said; and then he turned his back on me, to show the interview was ended, and began sifting through a stack of proofslips.

The first thing I did after I got outdoors was to send my wife a telegram saying that I had found a place at a moderate salary —I didn't dare tell her the size of the salary in a wire; I preferred to break that blow in a letter—and then I treated myself to a good cigar and sat in City Hall Park and smoked it. As I smoked I considered the outward aspect of the establishment where I was to work. When I got back to the boarding house there were three letters from three managing editors on my washstand—two letters from managing editors of morning papers and one letter from the managing editor of an evening paper—and all three were offering me trial jobs on the strength of that freak letter of mine!

By the evening mail also there came a note from Mr. Arthur Brisbane, of the *Journal,* saying that though he had no vacancies on his staff at present he would be glad to have me call upon him later, unless I found congenial employment elsewhere. By this I knew that my plan of interesting manag-

ing editors in my case by shocking them
had succeeded amply well. What I didn't
know was that, uniformly, morning papers
paid better salaries than evening papers, and
that, speaking by and large, a job as reporter on a morning paper carried or was
supposed to carry a little added prestige
and dignity—a distinction which, as I was to
learn subsequently, generally caused morning men and evening men to flock in separate camps when working together on the
same story. But even if I had known it I
think I would have stuck by my verbal contract to work for that shrewd-looking little
man. Already I liked his ways.

At eight o'clock the next morning I was
on hand, and so was he; and he greeted me
with his sad smile, which was chronic with
him. I had rather expected he would lead
me round the shop and introduce me to
everybody. He did nothing of the kind.
"We'll try you out and see where you fit in
best," he explained. "I believe you said you
knew something about editing telegraph."
He took me to where a half-bald, prema-
turely old young man was digging into

sheets of yellow flimsy and went through a brief and mumbling formality of introducing us. The bald-headed man didn't offer to shake hands. He considered me sourly, as though he had already contracted an intense aversion to me and would probably never be able to get over it; but he hospitably pushed the glue pot to the middle of the table and put his shears where I could reach them; then went on doing whatever he was doing. Considerably abashed I sat down in a chair that chanced to be on the opposite side of the table from him and awaited events. He found time to paste up a style sheet for me, showing the sizes of the heads and their proper designations; and he also briefly outlined the office rules for handling copy. They were mercifully few and amazingly sane.

Pretty soon after that he began to let me edit a few unimportant dispatches. I noticed, though, he kept all the worth-while stuff on his side of the table. Presently I caught him growling something in an undertone; and by listening hard I made out that he was addressing his remarks to me.

He was telling me what a rotten hole was this place that I had come to—how poor the pay was; how inefficient and unreasonable most of the heads of departments were; and how thankless and laborious was the job he himself held down. "There's only one decent thing to be said for this shop," he went on; "when a man makes halfway good here they don't fire him. Most of the other afternoon shops change staffs every ten minutes—we hold on to ours, bad as it is."

What he said worried me for the time being, as naturally it would; but before very long I found out that this bald pessimist was merely displaying, in a somewhat violent and advanced form, the symptoms of a most common complaint.

Inside the office, among his own office mates, it is the privilege of every newspaper man in New York to curse the entire organization with great frequency and the utmost freedom. Outside the office it is his pride to brag of his own paper, to defend its editors and staff in strong, unsalted speech, and to work his head off to keep it from being beaten.

While my new table mate was libeling the shop, I was taking in the shop. There was none of the feverish activity, none of the mad running to and fro, none of the howling aloud, that you read about in fiction stories of city newspaper life and see acted out in newspaper plays on the stage. As a matter of sober truth it should be said that the city room which runs the quietest is the one that is run the best. In a really good organization, such as this one was, the place became sanest when the stress became greatest. A good city staff is like a trained battleship crew—when trouble comes each man knows his place and his duty; and he goes to that place and attends to his duty with the least possible noise and excitement. He needs all his powers of concentration, without wasting them in vain shouts and ragtime evolutions.

On the day I am speaking of nobody at all seemed to be working hard. Between stints the copy readers read papers and wrote letters, the copy boys skylarked in

their corner and the reporters in sight mainly had their feet on their desks, their coats
off, and their pipes in their mouths. Occasionally the city editor would call one of
them, and the man he called would put on
his coat and saunter out, or else he would
slip into a telephone booth and emerge presently with a swatch of scribbled sheets in
his hand. I was surprised at this. In a
country office all hands would have been
gaited at a much higher speed. After a
while, though, when I had seen the tightening up that preceded going to press with an
edition, I appreciated the system that permitted men to loaf when the loafing was
good, to the end that they might be able to
hit mightier licks in emergencies.

I edited telegraph in small and inconse-
quential batches for two days. On the third
day I was taken away from my low-spirited
friend, much to his apparent relief, and set
to work writing an advance story, from file
clippings, of a naval review that would take
place the following week. I turned myself
loose on that story, giving a whole day to
it practically. When it was done I rather

fancied that it was well done; but next day, when it came out in the paper, I was pained to note that it had been cut to a commonplace, straight-away narrative. Practically all my fancy flights and neatly turned phrases had been killed out bodily. This was to happen to me several times before I learned my lesson, which was that almost universally copy readers in New York resent any effort on the part of a new hand to do any of this so-called fine writing. If a man with a fixed reputation comes on the paper to do writing of a certain sort, that is a different thing—mainly the copy desk will pass his copy as it stands; but it behooves the new and the unknown man to stick to the plainest and most unornamental English until he is established.

On the fourth day there was a substitute man on the city desk, the regular city editor having gone away on his vacation. About ten o'clock in the morning the understudy, who had sent most of his staff out on details of one sort or another, glanced about the room in a worried sort of fashion, hesitated a bit and hailed me.

"Here!" he said as I came over to him. "There's a general strike threatened on the L lines. The story may break any time. Cover it, will you?"

He handed me a couple of clippings from morning papers and then without another word turned away. By that time I had begun to acquire a few rudiments of office etiquette. For one thing, I knew that it wasn't good form to ask for explicit instructions from the man who handed out an assignment. You were presumed to know how to handle the contract whether you did or did not. And most certainly I did not. But I didn't expose my ignorance—not there anyhow.

I stuffed the clipping into my pocket and skipped down the spiral iron stairs and out into the human millrace of Park Row, and stood there for a minute with my thoughts in a jumble of confusion. By then I had begun vaguely to understand that news in New York was not gathered as news is gathered in most small cities—that instead of going from point to point on a given route, picking up what he might find, a man had a certain fixed post—headquarters, or the morgue, or the Harlem office, or the Brooklyn office, or somewhere—where he waited until orders came by telephone or otherwise to go out and cover specifically some story developing inside his own territory. That, however, applied to the station men and to the routine of the news. This story of mine plainly was out of the routine, and so must be undertaken in a different way. But what was it?

To give me time to catch my breath and take my bearings I climbed up on a shoeshiner's stand, and while the Greek youth worked over my shoes I read the clippings. Among things less definite, they told me that there might be a conference at the office of the general manager of the threatened lines some time during the forenoon. As a starter I decided to go to the general manager's office. After a little trouble I found it, half a mile away on an upper floor of the old Western Union Building, at Broadway and Dey Street. On a venture I sent my personal card in to the general manager, and his secretary came out to the anteroom where I stood and asked my business with his superior. I told him I was a reporter. He looked at me curiously, as though I must be a new variety of the species—as indeed I was; and then he told me the general manager had nothing to say for publication just then. As I turned away he halted me.

"Possibly you'd better wait round a bit," he hinted. "Later on there might be something you would want."

Having nothing better to do, I waited round. Various persons passed in and out; and in about ten minutes there came in, together, five men. By certain unmistakable marks of their craft I recognized them as reporters, but there was one thing about them that puzzled and rather startled me— the average age of the five. In the towns where I had worked reporters almost invariably were young chaps; generally they were men still in their early twenties. When a man reached, say, thirty he had either risen to the dignity of some inside job or else he had gone into some other business. But two out of this group were middle-aged, and one was downright elderly—he had a gray mustache, and his hair, what there was of it, was almost white. Later on I was to comprehend that here I beheld one of the big tragedies, perhaps the biggest tragedy, of the New York newspaper game.

Aside from the fascination of the calling itself, the thing that lures many a young fellow just out of college into newspaper work is the certainty that if he shows aptitude and adaptability he can within a year or two be earning his forty or his fifty or his sixty dollars a week, and be having a bully, fine exciting time while earning it. But the sad part of it is that, unless he develops a talent for some special line of newspaper endeavor or shows the executive instinct that lands him in an editorial berth, he is still at thirty earning what he earned at twenty. At forty he is probably earning even less than he did at thirty, and a newer generation of reporters is growing up round him and calling him "Pop." But if rum or irregular living doesn't get him it is a foregone conclusion that his enthusiasm will

last until he dies, because this trade of being
a reporter fastens on a man.

There is the endlessly shifting succession
of interesting jobs to handle; the constant
change of base and action; the fact that
never are two days exactly alike; and, most
of all, there is the personal equation of vanity and self-interest to be reckoned, since in
their own little world each man's work is
balanced daily against that of his fellows.
These things keep a reporter young in his
enthusiasms after his hair turns white and
his kneejoints rust. He may grow callous
to human emotions, even though maintain-
ing a certain artificial sympathy for purely
professional uses; he may grow cynical—
next to policemen, city newspaper men are
the most skeptical people on earth, I reckon
—but the fine fire of his youthful ardor will
burn always.

Three of the five men who entered now
were of this young-old type that I learned
to know so well later. The fourth was a
nondescript, a suit of clothes wrapped round
a nonentity; but the fifth, a chubby, blue-
eyed, youthful-looking chap, was plainly

the leader of the group. They collected in a corner, with the air of having nothing in particular to do, and I wormed my way into the circle and told them I was a reporter too.

The youngest of the lot looked at me keenly.

"New man—huh?" he asked.

I told him "Yes."

"I thought so," he said, and went on talking to the others.

I made myself small and quiet. Presently the secretary came, with duplicates enough to go round of a statement the general manager had prepared. Each man glanced through his carbon copy and then the leader said: "Strike headquarters next—eh?" They all seemed to agree with him and then made off, going, when they got outside, in different directions, being bound, as I discovered later, for the nearest telephone pay-stations. As for me I went back to my office, prepared to write something and incorporate the statement in it. The acting city editor seemed slightly surprised to see me; and, to my surprise, he wouldn't let me write anything.

"You're doing the leg work on this story," he said, "and you'd better not lose any more time getting back on the job. Turn over what you've got to Keefe, yonder—he'll write it—and you hustle right back on the assignment. And don't come in with what you get—telephone it in!"

This was my abrupt introduction to the system by which most of the live news is handled for the New York evening newspapers and, in a measure, for the morning papers too—a system of which I had never heard before. Its continued use has bred up two distinct and separate types of news-specialists—the leg man, who gets the story, but rarely writes it; and the rewrite man, who writes the story, but rarely gets it. A combination of causes is responsible for its development—the growth of the city, with its increasing distances; the need of haste to meet the editions that pile out one upon the other's heels; and, most of all, the universal spread of the telephone. To my mind the uniform precision with which it works out is the most marvelous single feature of that most marvelous of human mechanisms—a New York evening newspaper. It enables a paper to accomplish the seemingly impossible six days a week and many times a day.

Let a big story break—a fire, a crime, anything where the action is hurried and unexpected—and the leg man is promptly on hand. Within the quickest possible passage of time he collects his stuff, a scrap here and a scrap there, until he has enough to make a coherent and connected narrative. Then he dives for a near-by telephone and over the wire pours out his tale to the rewrite man, who, hunched up in a soundproof booth at the other end of the wire, is taking notes as fast as his pencil can skip. If he is a good leg man he supplies something besides the mere recital of names and facts—in quick illuminating sentences he draws a picture that makes the rewrite man see the thing himself. This done, the rewrite man jumps for his typewriter and rattles off the story, a paragraph at a time; very often from the depths of his own imagination he draws the flashes of humor, the

darting touches of local color, the nuggets
of graphic description, which lift that particular story out of the ruck and make it
fairly sizzle with life and movement.

In my opinion the best police reporter
in New York is a certain stolid, quiet man
of fifty-five or thereabout. His sense of
news values is a part of him. He knows
what details to play up; by instinct seemingly he knows invariably how to begin his
story over the telephone and when to leave
off; he never wastes an unnecessary word
nor leaves out a necessary one. Nearly always, if the rewrite man puts the story together in the order in which he got it from
this man, he will make no mistake—the
story in print will be right. Through writing his stories as he sent them in, three men
I have in mind made reputations that enabled them to graduate out of newspaper
work into connections with leading magazines. Yet in all his thirty-five years as a
police reporter this man has never with his
own hand written a single line for publication in a newspaper. Inversely, some of
the strongest and most effective stories of big

news events—stories that made people talk and caused them to write letters to editors —were done by rewrite men sitting in cluttered offices miles away from the places where the events occurred.

Within an hour I was to get another needed lesson in the business of reporting in New York. I surrendered my notes to the waiting Keefe, dusted out and hurried up to a hotel near the Grand Central Station where the labor leaders were in session; and for the first time I found out that, when covering a big story, the men representing the various papers work together, each sharing with all the others what he independently may learn. If a man is caught holding back some valuable detail that one act of double-dealing ends his usefulness and destroys his standing. The other men will conspire against him and intrigue against him, and plot to deceive and mislead him until they drive him out of his job. Moreover, if a man for any reason save sheer laziness falls down on his assignment the other men will protect his paper from a beating, and by protecting it will protect him. In the towns where I had worked before we had a different code—there it was every man for himself always. Here it was every man for every other man, all for one and one for all.

City editors rail against these news combines, but it was the instinct of self-preservation that long ago drove the leg men into tight and fast organizations. They learned that an exclusive news coup—a beat as it is called in the East or a scoop in the West— is praised to-day and forgotten to-morrow; but the man who scores a beat to-day, and to-morrow gets beaten, maybe will lose his job. So, regardless of their personal and private feelings for one another, the reporters stand together. This is in a measure a trade secret—telling it here may unravel a puzzle for persons who have perhaps wondered why, when a big news story comes along, each paper in each edition will have the same facts that all the other papers have —no more and no less.

I didn't know all this, however, on that day when I hustled uptown to cover the strikers' end of the L strike story; and my ignorance came very near getting me into disrepute right at the outset. The pursuit of facts led us to the residence of Mr. August Belmont, the head of the Interborough system, where, as we learned somehow, a secret conference of the two factions interested in the threatened trouble was due to take place. I was told off to stand guard at the front door, in case any one should come out. The blue-eyed, chubby-cheeked chap, who by common consent acted as leader of our forces, went with one of the older reporters down to the corner, to intercept a prominent labor union official who was expected to arrive from that direction at any minute.

Presently, as I idled about the stoop of Mr. Belmont's house, watching my new associates out of the tail of my eye, I saw them halt their man. Possibly in the hope of shaking them off, he turned and started away; they kept pace with him. My previous training had taught me that what a reporter got himself he kept himself; so, fearing that I was about to miss some important phase of the story, I ran after them and caught up with them. The blue-eyed chap stopped dead still and gave me a tongue lashing for deserting my post.

"Say, you!" he said. "Don't you know you'll get anything that we find out just as soon as any of the fellows get it? Now you go back there and stay where I put you!"

During the rest of the day he snubbed me unmercifully, but he didn't let me overlook any detail of value; and under his careful guidance I covered the story creditably that day and for all the rest of the week.

For quite a spell after this I did leg work mostly; and, though I didn't exactly fall down on any of my assignments, yet it seemed to me I didn't go ahead very fast. But my salary was advanced five dollars at a time until it amounted to thirty dollars a week. I wasn't able to get anything distinctive into the paper either—the ever vigilant copy readers attended to that—and plenty of times I was discouraged and sorehearted. Looking back on it now, though, I know this experience was worth a good deal to me, because all the time, by assiduously looking and listening and by copying others, I was making over my preconceived ideas of what constitutes news to conform with the New York standard, which, in nearly all its essentials, is entirely different from the small-town standard. Also, I was learning the city thoroughly. On street cars or afoot, but mainly afoot, I toured Manhattan Island from end to end and from side to side, studying streets, studying crowds, studying types, studying signboards, show windows, house-fronts, fire-escapes—studying whatever was interesting; and that meant everything I saw.

I had abundant time for this sort of thing, for outside of working hours I was most desperately lonely. The other men in the office all appeared to have private affairs of their own to concern them, and they left me pretty much alone. I had looked in vain for the Bohemian newspaper man who, I had been led to suppose, was so common a type in New York. All my life I had been deluded by a notion that newspaper men in New York were a carefree, reck-

less, gifted, irresponsible, dashing race, who
regularly fraternized together over mugs
of musty ale in fascinating little dramshops.
Perhaps there was a time when this condition existed, but personally I don't believe
it ever did.

It is true that, outside his office, a New
York newspaper man may lead pretty much
the sort of life he fancies; and, so long as
he attends to his duties, neither his employers, his superiors, nor his associates will
feel called upon to regulate his private
moralities for him.   The strange discipline
of the place, which appears so slack and
irregular to the onlooker, and which is in
reality so rigid and exacting, doesn't follow him after he puts on his hat and coat at
quitting time; but he cannot drink to excess
and expect to get ahead or to stay ahead.
Newspaper owners do not want drunkards
on their staffs any more than successful men
in any other line of business want them.
Real newspaper men in New York are never
Bohemians, and they despise men who pose
as Bohemians.   They are mainly hard-working, steady-paced persons, with families to

support; and when they get through work they go home to their families and stay there. So my youthful rural dreams of mingling with those carefree and fascinating geniuses in beer cellars never came true.

As for the people in my boarding house, they appeared to me to be a commonplace and uninteresting lot, taking them on the average. Besides, I had already contracted the newspaper man's worst disease, which is the fault of being interested only in his own trade and what pertains to it. So it befell that, in the office or out, I kept to myself, being troubled with frequent doubts as to my future. I worried, too, over my failure to get ahead with the promptness I had counted on. I reckon I was pretty tolerably homesick too—those first few months. A stranger's first half year in New York is apt to be about the most miserable period of his existence anyhow. After that time, if he has any human qualities, he finds his place and fits himself into it; and life begins to be worth something to him in companionship. But those first six months—ouch! It is my experience a man can be lonelier and bluer, and can feel more forsaken in the midst of five million people than he ever could on a desert island. I've never tried the desert island, but know about the five millions.

Along toward winter the management of the paper decided to try the experiment of putting the first edition upon the streets at eight o'clock in the morning instead of waiting until ten. In Park Row parlance the staff that gets out this 8 A. M. edition is known as the lobster trick. A man assigned to that shift says he is working on the lobster. When our paper followed a lead that had already proved reasonably successful in the case of two or three rival papers, I was selected to edit the lobster edition—the thanks for this being due largely to my previously acquired knowledge of headlining and copy reading. At the same time my salary was raised five dollars a week.

I earned it all right—I had to get up at one-thirty o'clock in the morning in order to reach the office at two, when the work started. I hated the hours; it was a frightful wrench to roll out of a warm bed into the middle of a winter night. Every time that accursed alarm clock went off I roused with the feeling that I had been asleep fifteen minutes. I got to know the unhappy sensations of that proverbial early riser— the condemned man of a rural hanging story. Yet in a way I enjoyed holding the new post. I had a measure of responsibility upon me—I was giving a few orders instead of taking a great many, and I was seeing the city in those dun-colored hours before the dawn, when those who stay up to meet the sun mingle with those who get up to meet it; when the outcast, the criminal, and the homeless, the roisterer, the waster and the profligate—the classes who never work and the classes who never quit working —come together to form one of the saddest, most moving pictures you can ever hope— or fear—to see. And, besides, it was through this new employment that I got my first chance really to make good.

Getting to work at two in the morning and quitting at eight gave me more leisure

than I had before even. From the office
I would go back to the boarding house
and sleep until noon, provided two young
women practicing music scales on the floor
below would let me. From noon on, then,
the day was mine. On my income I couldn't
afford matinées—especially as I was sending half of my salary to my wife—and as I
had made mighty few friends my afternoons
might have been unbearably long and
dreary if I hadn't kept busy.

Regularly all through that winter I
worked two hours a day on my play. It
is agreed, I take it, that every newspaper
man writes at least one play in his life. So
I wrote mine. It has never been played and
it never will be played; but, nevertheless,
I wrote it and rewrote it, and wrote it over
again six times. Probably because I was
still homesick I laid the scenes of it in my
home town, and all the characters were
home folks. Sitting there in my eight-by-
ten quarters, with my feet on a gas-stove
about as big as a pocket inkstand, I peopled
that hall bedroom with pictures of back-
home types; and into their mouths I put the

familiar speech of a border Southern community. It was a pretty sad sort of play, as I know now; but I contend yet that it contained a number of accurate likenesses.

As I was saying, I would write two hours a day on the play. Then I would go out and roam the streets until dusk. At six I would eat my dinner and by seven I would be in bed; but, as I didn't work Sundays, on Saturdays I would continue my voyages of exploration until late at night. One Saturday night I made a tour of the dance-halls in the Tenderloin. There was one particular dance-hall, a dingy basement dive in a side street just off Broadway, which by reason of its unrelieved sordidness and vulgarity made an especially deep impression upon me. I stayed there an hour or more, watching the habitués in their dreary, heartbreaking task of trying to act as though they were enjoying themselves.

On the following Tuesday, at three o'clock in the morning, a murder occurred in this same place—a murder marked by features so dramatic and so unusual as to lift it out of the class of ordinary Tenderloin murders. Our early trick man at head-quarters got there before the blood of the two victims was dry upon the floor, and by telephone he sent in a corking good account; and I took his story off the telephone. The picture of the dingy little boozing den was still fresh in my memory. I had the local color of it right where I could put my hands on it, so, instead of turning the notes over to the lone rewrite man of my shift, I wrote the story myself. And, though I say it myself, it was a good story. My mind was full of newly formed impressions of Tenderloin honk-a-tonks and I think I wrote the story in a new way. It was a better story than I shall ever be able to do again on the same subject.

Moreover, having written the story myself, I edited it myself. There was no earnest-minded butcher of a copy reader there, with his deadly blue pencil, to carve the life out of it. It went into the first edition just as I wrote it, and it ran all day on the front page, holding its position through the subsequent editions. It attracted attention in our office; and what for my purposes was a better thing it attracted attention in near-by offices. There is just one thing that a New York city editor reads with more care than he reads his own paper—and that's the other fellow's paper. On the popularity of that story I got offers of jobs from two city editors who had never heard of me before; and, at last, I knew I had broken in. I had proof of it when my paper shortly thereafter sent me up to Portsmouth to help cover the Peace Conference.

It is a good long time now since I came to New York; but, as I look back on it, it doesn't seem more than a few months. Most of what I write now is printed in a magazine, but I'm still a reporter and I expect to be a reporter always. It's a good, clean trade—being a reporter is—and I'm proud to call myself one. I've only one regret—I waited until I was nearly twenty-eight years old to break into New York. I only wish I had done it at eighteen.

Stickfuls

IN AND OUT OF THE CITY ROOM
CHAPTER FOUR

Inside Stories

CHAPTER IV

Inside Stories

WHEN the last trump sounds and the quick and the dead come trooping up to be weighed in the balance for their deeds in the flesh I expect to be there along with the rest of the tribe of fictionists. There ought to be quite a crowd of us. The inheritors of the mantle of O. Henry alone should require at least half an hour to pass a given point, though most of them will be invisible by reason of being completely hidden under the mantle. When my time comes to undergo cross-examination before the judgment seat humbly shall I admit:

"I have been guilty of many a crime of literary omission and many a crime of literary commission. I have left undone the things which I should have done and I have done the things which I should not have done. Many a time and oft have I hauled off and given the poor old English grammar a wallop on the point of the jaw. But in extenuation for all these, my manifold shortcomings, I may plead this: I never wrote the story of the burglar who broke into a home on Christmas Eve and was mistaken by a little che-ild for Santa Claus. I never wrote the story of the prodigal son who returned from the Klondike, laden with gold, just in time to pay off the mortgage on the old homestead and thus save his aged parents from being dispossessed into a bitter snowstorm.

"I never wrote the story of the intoxicated tramp who, in his tatters, wandered into a fancy-dress ball and won the prize for the most effective costume.

"I never wrote the story of the substitute football player who was thrust into the game at the fifty-fifth minute of the eleventh hour, and who—being inspired by a vision of his sweetheart's face—tied the score and saved the day by making a phenomenal run round the end. Several times, I confess, I have been tempted to write this story, but was each time saved by the reflection that so many others already had done it so well.

"And I never wrote the story of the down-trodden squab reporter who scooped the town on the most important news story of the year, thereby plastering shame upon the face of the cruel city editor with the rasping voice and the soul of a hard-boiled egg. Of these acts of forbearance, the last I deem to be the greatest and the most commendable of all.

"In conclusion I would state that I wear a seven and three-eighths halo and I figure I shall require an oversized set of wings, with a spread of at least fourteen feet from tip to tip. Where do I go to get my harp?"

I suppose the principal reason why I never wrote the story of the cub reporter and the mean city editor was because I have been a cub reporter in my time, and also I have been a city editor, and I knew better than to write it, strong though the provocation to do so may have been on occasion. In twenty-odd years of experience in active daily newspaper work I had personal knowledge of but one instance of a callow fledgling achieving a really notable news beat, and then he did it, not through merit and not through intelligence on his part, but by virtue of a stroke of luck which fell upon him like a thunderbolt. I speak with authority here because I was that reporter. I have known only one city editor who essayed the rôle of a Simon Legree, and he failed to play the part successfully, because by nature he was rather a kindly and a well-disposed person. Indeed, as I recall, he rounded out his career by becoming the publicity agent for a charity organization specializing in child welfare.

All the same, though I have not dared write this popular perennial, I love to read it, because it is so familiar to me and because at first glance I recognize all the old favorite props and because I know in advance substantially how it is going to turn out.

Another thing I like to do is to go to a play in which there is an act or a scene purporting to show the city room of a metropolitan newspaper, filled with noise and excitement and mad outcries and the sound of pelting feet, with the newspaper about to go to press and the principal characters casually happening in one after another further to clutter up the stage, and the noble hero dashing in a minute and a half before the curtain with the information which saves the reputation of his fiancée's father, or else with the exposure which will confound the corrupt political boss.

The reason why I like this scene so much is because what it portrays is so teetotally different from what any real city room is at press time. It is evidence of the heights to which a dramatist's imagination may rise when he is not hampered by actualities but can let his fancy rove wild and free.

One trouble with most of us who write stories for a living is that we are creatures of habit and prone to follow along the line of least resistance. Years and years ago some inspired romancer, casting about for a new way to phrase a plain statement, wrote, "For Egbert to reach the window of the opposite side of the room was but the work of a moment," instead of stating that Egbert quickly crossed the room to the window. And ever since the race of writers has been using the same hackneyed method of expressing a straightaway fact in a round-about fashion.

I don't know who it was who first struck upon the notion of using the verb "gutter" in conjunction with the noun "candle," but I do know that a whole generation of us have described candles as guttering. I've done it myself any number of times, and yet right now if you ask me point-blank what a candle does when it gutters or how it looks when it gutters I shall have to be excused from answering.

A couple of decades back a novelist, or perhaps it was a short-story writer or possibly a playwright, visioned the typical captain of finance as a middle-aged man with iron-gray hair and a square jaw and a brusque manner who forever was puffing on a large black cigar; this as counter-distinguished from the English writer's American millionaire, who invariably wore chin whiskers and spat tobacco juice on strange people's carpets and said "I calculate" and "I guess" and constantly bragged of the money he had. The native conception endured for upward of twenty years; indeed it only passed out of vogue at a comparatively recent time, when a modern writer, subtly sensing that his public had grown weary of captains of finance with iron-gray hair and square jaws and harsh ways and fat black cigars, audaciously leaped to the other extreme and presented him to the buyers of best sellers as a small, shrinking figure with a thin sandpiperish voice who never smoked anything stronger than a cubeb cigarette.

Of course fiction writers in their essential intellectual processes are not different from the run of humanity about them; and if the experience of the centuries has taught us anything at all it has taught us that mankind would rather think in a groove than think at large and at random, because the former is easier and the result more likely to conform to popular ideals and popular precedents.

Possibly I am saying what follows because I know more of the actual workings of a city newspaper shop than I know of the inside of any other business, but it has always seemed to me that there was a greater volume of current misinformation abroad regarding newspapers than regarding any main industry in our country. The fault for this, if I am one to judge, lies in two reasons: First, certain venerable misconceptions regarding the methods employed in news gathering have been told so often they have become hallowed by repetition; and second, because story writers and dramatists, either through ignorance or because the desire to depict the dramatic led them far astray from the verities, have persistently followed certain formulas.

Be the main cause what it may, certain illusions, all of them woefully incorrect and most of them entirely false, firmly have been grafted upon the lay mind, to wit:

That practically all city editors are crabbed misanthropists with the dispositions of a dyspeptic Nero.

That all newspapers are terribly put to it to find material with which to fill up their columns.

That reporters are nosey youths, armed with large notebooks, who prowl about town on the lookout for something exciting or unusual to happen so that they may hurry back to their offices and write overdrawn pieces about it.

That a reporter will go to any ends in order to get hold of a piece of news which a brother reporter has not yet got hold of, and that having got it he will die in his tracks before he will whack up with his fellow.

That a reporter who gets a story—the word being here used in the newspaper sense to imply anything which is printable, from a paragraph to a page article—invariably writes it out himself for publication.

That the sap-green reporter invariably lands the biggest beat.

That a newspaper shop is run like a madhouse, and that as the hour of going to press approaches it becomes more of a madhouse than ever, being peopled with agitated figures rushing wildly to and fro and uttering demoniac shrieks.

That all the old-time newspaper stars were habitual drunkards and did their best work while in a state of staggering intoxi-

cation. Also that many of the brilliant figures of the present day are cursed with the
same craving for strong waters and are suffered by their employers to lead dissipated
lives because they are most sparkling when
they are most soused.

At the risk of destroying popular belief
in these revered traditions it seems to me it
might not be amiss to sprinkle the mass with
a few grains of truth. As already I have
intimated, city editors uniformly are not
cold-eyed despots tyrannizing over frightened crews. The best city editor I ever
worked for rarely raised his voice above a
gentle conversational pitch except when he
was cursing his own mistakes.

For every line of copy that a newspaper
puts into type it throws away many lines.
Nine-tenths of the stuff which reaches a
newspaper office goes promptly into a waste-
basket. The difficulty usually is not to find
sufficient material with which to fill up
space but to cut down the supply to a point
where what is timely and what is interesting and what is vital in the news may be
cramped and crowded and compressed into

each edition. This applies not only to the news, but on frequent occasion to paid advertising matter. Because of a standing rule that the proportion of advertising shall be at a given ratio to the proportion of straight reading matter appearing along with it, a metropolitan newspaper publisher very often throws out of a single issue thousands of dollars' worth of advertising. This always has been true, and particularly is it true at present when print paper is so scarce.

This brings us down to Count Three of the indictment: The city reporter does not carry a fat notebook with him, or if he does carry it he does not haul it out while on duty; neither does he wander about vaguely looking for things to happen. Either he is a district man, so called, assigned to a designated beat and never leaving his beat except under orders from his chief, or he is an assignment man covering one particular assignment at a time and not especially concerned with anything else which may come to his attention, unless that thing pertains in some fashion or other to the task in hand.

Under the modern system of reporting in the larger cities the reporter who goes out to get a story does not often write the story himself. Generally he telephones the details to his shop, and a specialist takes down the facts and prepares the copy for publication. The outside man, the one who is sent to cover the story, is called a leg man. The inside expert is known as a rewrite man.

Oftener than not the graphic account which you read of a fire or an accident was hammered on a typewriter by a man sitting at a desk miles away from the spot where the event occurred. He has developed to a high degree the knack of setting down in black and white things viewed through another man's eyes.

The belief that a reporter is happiest when he is scooping his fellow reporter is one of the commonest assumptions held by those who have never been reporters, and one of the most erroneous possible. In practically all the larger cities in this country reporters work together. A certain code governs their confederacy. If a group of reporters representing different papers are working on the same news story each is in honor bound to divide with his fellows any and every legitimate item of information which comes into his possession for so long as he is detailed to the assignment.

The customary procedure is to devise a rough working plan wherein the men, singly or in pairs, cover separate ends of the story, each being under an implied pledge—which rarely is violated—to keep his confrères posted to the minute regarding the developments which have come to his attention and of which naturally the others might know nothing unless he did advise them. If he cannot get in touch with an associate in time for the other man to catch an edition with the details he has just secured he will telephone to the office where his associate is employed and report direct.

If this were not the case, every metropolitan paper would be compelled to employ a city staff unwieldy and expensive beyond belief. Moreover a sense of self-protection upon the part of the reporters themselves enters into the equation. If a reporter, working under agreement with one or more members of his trade, breaks the faith he becomes a marked man. The word goes out that So-and-So has thrown down the crowd, and immediately the rest of the fraternity conspires at the next chance to punish him for his transgression by withholding from him essential facts otherwise held as common property.

Moreover experience has taught the reporter that in the long run it will avail him little to pull off a beat at the expense of his supposed rivals, because by day after tomorrow the achievement will be forgotten even in his own city room, whereas the next time he misses an important development he is in for a scolding or something worse.

Like most good rules, this rule is flexible and has its exceptions. For example, this would be a typical exception: Six reporters, let us say, serving six newspapers are at work on a story presenting various ramifications. To one of them comes—not through the regular and recognized news channels but through outside sources—a hint which promises possibilities.

Perhaps while he is off duty he meets an acquaintance who tells him of an interesting side light which has a bearing upon the case but which has not cropped up along beaten paths. Perhaps a member of his own staff gets hold of the tip and passes it along to him.

With the utmost frankness he tells the other five men that he is off to dig up what promises to be an exclusive end of the story. None of them spies on him, none of them expects him to divulge the facts he may secure while following this private lead. They all understand, and so do their city editors, that it has been his fortune to strike an unknown and previous unsuspected trail, and that the business is his business and not theirs.

Not often is a cub reporter permitted to handle an important factor in an important news event. In the first place he probably wouldn't know what to do with a big news story if he ran on one. His is a trade which has to be learned, just as every other trade does. In the second place there nearly always is a journeyman reporter within reach of the city editor when big news breaks, and no sane city editor would assign an apprentice to a task of importance when he has master craftsmen at his beck and call. The callow beginner who, unaided and working against the handicaps of an unappreciative taskmaster at the city desk and self-sufficient, patronizing veterans in the city room, pulls off a monumental scoop, is to be found only in fiction. That, I may add, is exactly where he belongs, seeing that he is the figment either of a fiction-writer's imagination or of a fiction-writer's impulse to use stock models.

There may have been a day when great newspaper reporters were great drunkards, but I'll say this: It was before my day. A certain discipline, which is all the more exact and all the more exacting because on the surface it seems scarcely to exist at all, regulates the interior economies of a properly conducted city room. A modern newspaper no more desires to have a congenital drunkard on its staff than a bank presi-

early days of yellow journalism, there was a newspaper manager, one of the pioneers of the saffron cult, who confused tumult with enthusiasm and mistook vain noise for proof of zeal; but he didn't last long. His proprietor caught onto him, as Walter Pater would say, and cast him into the outer darkness, or else made an exchange editor of him, which comes to the same thing. These times any functionary in a city room whether it were the managing editor or the news editor or the make-up editor or the head of the copy desk or so on right down the line to the newest office boy, who shrieked and raved when there was no occasion for shrieking and raving—and there never is any such occasion—who leaped from crag to crag as some character is forever doing in a stage newspaper office, would shortly find himself enrolled in the great army of the unemployed.

The first story to which I was assigned after I had come to New York and had got a job on an evening paper was a threatened strike of the Interborough trainmen. The principal properties then owned by the Interborough were the elevated roads, but the first subway had just been completed and was about to be opened. The certainty that the strike—if it came—would delay the long-promised beginning of operations in the subway gave an added note of interest and apprehension to the prospective tie-up.

For sufficient reasons of his own, Mr. August Belmont, the head of the system, was doing his best to evade the newspaper men. I remember that a squad of us spent a whole day tracking him down. We hunted him from his house to the house of Mr. J. Pierpont Morgan, where he took part in a conference of some sort; thence to national Democratic headquarters—this was the year of the Roosevelt-Parker campaign; thence to his club, where he ate lunch; thence to the executive offices of the Interborough in a building on Dey Street, downtown; and finally late in the afternoon we trapped him in his own offices on the east side of Broadway in the Wall Street district.

In each separate movement Mr. Belmont had done his level best to confuse the trail,

stories on the same subject done by other men and by these gauges of comparison to decide wherein he excelled or wherein he failed to take full advantage of the opportunity presented to him. It largely is the personal equation, which in the last analysis means the equation of vanity, which inspires him to take any risks, to endure any hardships, to go without his meals and his sleep, in order to attain his ends.

Had Mr. Belmont been running a newspaper instead of a transit system I dare say he would have found his staff to be permeated with the same zest for work which he professed to admire in us.

I know of no profession wherein chances for individual initiative, for the exercise of the ability to think quickly and to act as quickly, are so frequent. I recall an instance in point: Some years ago a man waylaid Postmaster Morgan, of New York, on his way from his home to the subway and shot him down, then shot himself. The postmaster, though badly wounded, recovered. His assailant died instantly. A citizen thought he recognized in the dead man a neighbor of his in Harlem, and this claim was published in the extras which appeared on the street within less than an hour after the shooting. A little later, though, it developed that the citizen had made a mistake and that the suicide was really an erratic-mannered stranger who had been occupying a furnished room in lodgings uptown.

Quite by chance a reporter for the paper on which I was employed stumbled upon the fact of the correct identification. The police knew it, but for reasons best known to themselves were endeavoring for the time to suppress it. This reporter, whom we may call Sheridan, set out hotfoot for the house where the assassin had been living, reaching there in advance of the detectives. The proprietor of the establishment, a woman, answered his knock at the door.

"I want to examine the room of one of your boarders," he told her. "A little while ago he shot a man and then killed himself. His name is believed to be So-and-So."

"I'm sorry, mister," said the woman, "but I can't let you in. I just had a tele-

phone message from the police telling me
what had happened and ordering me to
admit nobody to his room until officers from
the station house could get here. They particularly said I was not to let any reporters
in."

Hesitation on the reporter's part would
have been as fatal to the success of his plan
as argument would have been. He neither
hesitated nor argued. Taking recourse in a
somewhat common subterfuge, he threw
back the lapel of his coat and gave the
woman an instantaneous glimpse at the fire
badge he wore pinned underneath.

"See that?" he said. "I'm not a reporter.
I'm from the coroner's office, and in a case
like this the coroner comes ahead of the
police even. It is my duty to examine the
personal effects of this man and it is your
duty to assist me in every way possible. If
you refuse you will be in danger of prosecution."

Without delay the woman admitted him.
She led him up the stairs to the shabby
room the stranger had occupied and un-
locked the door for him. In five minutes

Sheridan had found out what he wanted to know—namely, that the man was a homicidal maniac, a former inmate of an asylum, whose writings showed that for months he had been nursing an imaginary grudge against Postmaster Morgan. His perverted brain had been filled with the delusion that Morgan, as the head of a group of conspirators, had been plotting to withhold from him important private letters.

Sheridan sped round the corner to the nearest pay-telephone station and in half an hour we were on the streets with a second extra giving the real name of the assassin and the principal facts about him, the most important of these being the motive for his act. It was a clean beat.

Five minutes after Sheridan vanished another reporter, whom I shall call Stone, jumped out of a taxicab and hurried up the front steps of the lodging house. Stone, also a member of our staff, had been detailed independently to a more remote angle of the shooting. At a police station uptown a friendly desk sergeant whispered to him that the assassin had been staying at such-and-such an address, and Stone darted out and hailed a cab and hastened to the place, not knowing of course that Sheridan had been there ahead of him, but only knowing he must move swiftly if he expected to attain any results before policemen arrived afoot or by street car, probably with a queue of reporters behind them.

As in Sheridan's case, the landlady met Stone at the door and barred his way.

"Oh, that's all right, I'm the coroner," said Stone, resorting to the same deceit which his confrère had practiced.

"Is that so?' inquired the woman skeptically. "Well, it may interest you to know that the coroner has been here and gone."

"Yes, I know," said Stone; he was a quick thinker; "but the situation is this: There are two coroners in this part of town. I have the district lying to the south and the man who was just here has the district lying to the north. The middle of this street is the dividing line between the two districts. This house being on the south side of the street is in my district, and so the other coroner made a mistake and went outside of his own jurisdiction when he took charge of this case, which properly belongs to me and on which I must make a report or get into serious trouble."

"Yes, but the other man showed me his credentials," demurred the woman, only half convinced.

"What credentials did he show you?" demanded Stone.

"Why, he showed me his badge."

Out of Stone's pocket came his fire badge. He held it cupped in his hand so that the woman might make out its shape and yet not be able to read the lettering upon it.

"Was it a badge like this?" he asked.

"Yes," she admitted, "it was."

"Well, you see, don't you," he said, "that I have just as much authority to come in as the other man had?—more in fact because, as I've just explained to you, he accidentally went outside of his district into mine."

Completely disarmed of her suspicions, the woman admitted him, and when two detectives appeared they found him in the dead man's room going through the dead man's effects, which already had been hastily rummaged by Sheridan.

Sheridan has quit the newspaper business and is now an important figure in a big moving-picture concern. Stone is out of the game too. He died not so very long ago, leaving behind him a record crowded with reportorial achievements. Along Park Row they still recall memories of his shrewdness, his mental agility and his untiring energies when covering a story which appealed to his imagination and to that bloodhound instinct for nosing out obscure trails which all great reporters possess. They tell tales, too, of another side of his nature. He was by way of being an incurable practical joker.

Once upon a time Stone had charge of the Tenderloin office of one of the evening papers. His headquarters was in the heart of the theater and hotel district, then centering about Herald Square. On the other side of the street, and almost directly opposite, was the branch office of another evening paper. Over the way one morning there appeared a freshly recruited member of the

staff of the opposition sheet. The new-
comer was a tall Englishman who wore a
monocle and had a rich bah-Jove accent
such as rarely is heard off the burlesque
stage. I think it was this man's patronizing manner when he met Stone that afternoon, rather than his monocle or his accent,
which immediately roused on Stone's part
an antagonism for the Britisher, whose
name, let us say, was Slocum.

On the following day, first making sure
that Slocum was on waiting duty across the
street, he called up the opposition office
on the telephone and in a disguised voice
said he wished to speak to Slocum.

"This is the city desk downtown," he
stated when Slocum had answered. "We've
just got a tip here that the Duke of Devon-
shire is stopping at the Hotel Durham two
or three blocks from where you are now.
He's come over on some private mission.
Hurry right round to the Durham and insist
on seeing the duke and get a good snappy
interview with him. Find out if you can
what business he's here on."

"Yes, sir," said Slocum, flattered at being

Metropolitan newspaper traditions are dotted thick with annals of successful undertakings on the part of reporters who ferreted out crimes and criminals after the police had failed, but to my mind one of the most notable examples of high-grade detective work ever performed by a newspaper man has never been narrated except by word of mouth. The case at the outset briefly was this: A young man holding a responsible position with a large financial concern lived in a pretty cottage in an outlying suburban district of one of the subdivisions of a big Eastern city. Very early one morning he wakened his wife and told her he heard suspicious noises on the first floor and was going downstairs to investigate. He bade her stay where she was. He took a pistol and slipped down the steps.

A few moments later the wife, waiting above, heard a shot. She screamed for help, rousing the neighbors. A man who lived next door was the first to respond. Coming at top speed he found the front door standing open. He ran in and switched on the lights. The head of the house, shot through the body and dying, was stretched upon the floor of the dining room. His pistol, unfired, was near him. A second revolver, with one cartridge in it freshly discharged and with its barrel still warm from firing, also was lying close by the victim. On the table was a sheet containing silverware tied up in a bundle.

Further search on the part of residents in the vicinity and on the part of the policemen, when they arrived, resulted in the finding of a double trail of footprints, one set leading across the lawn and upon the porch to the door; the other set, spaced far apart as though made by a man running, led back again to the street. Muddied footprints corresponding in outline with those outside were thick upon the carpet in the room where the tragedy had occurred.

The police—and everybody else—advanced the theory that the householder, coming upon a burglar, had been shot down before he had had opportunity to use his own revolver. Going upon this plausible and apparently indisputable hypothesis, detectives scoured the neighborhood, round-ing up suspicious characters in wholesale lots and giving them one by one the third degree. A certain reporter, who since has obtained a wide reputation as a special writer, worked on the story. Even after popular interest in the tragedy had somewhat abated, and after search for the supposed murderer had taken on a perfunctory phase, he continued his investigations singlehanded. Privately he told his city editor he was not altogether satisfied with the views held by the police department, and the city editor having confidence in the young man's skill as an amateur sleuth told him to take as much time as he pleased for the private inquiry.

Within forty-eight hours thereafter the reporter jolted the town and the police force with sensational disclosures. The victim had not been killed by a house-breaking marauder. He had killed himself. He was in difficulties, though he had managed to keep his embarrassments secret. He carried life insurance for a considerable sum; the policy he had taken out a few months before. The policy contained the customary clause invalidating the insurance in the event the insured should willfully take his own life within a specified scope of time; and so in order that his widow might not be left without means the young man, with infinite care and detail, had planned an elaborate stage setting with a view to creating seemingly incontestable proof that he had died by violence at the hands of another.

Presumably in the early part of the night of the tragedy, while his wife lay sleeping, he had made the double series of telltale tracks, employing for the purpose a pair of shoes much larger than the size which he himself customarily wore. Likewise he had opened the front door, had tied up the silver in a sheet, and finally—after waking his wife—had gone downstairs and shot himself with a revolver procured in advance for that very contingency. The widow had believed he was murdered. The neighbors had believed it. The police all along had been absolutely convinced of it. Then why hadn't the reporter accepted what seemed on the surface of things a plain and provable state of facts?

Here's why: Shortly after he reached the spot—and that meant a very short time after the shooting—he talked with the citizen who had answered the first alarm. That man had said to him:

"Do you know, there's one peculiar feature about this awful thing. There's a pet fox terrier over next door, and when I ran in there after I heard the shot and after I heard Mrs. Blank scream the dog was standing right alongside his master. From all I can gather, the dog must have come downstairs with him when he first heard the burglar at work in the dining room.

"But the curious thing about it is that the dog didn't bark a single time after the shooting took place. And I am almost prepared to swear he didn't bark beforehand either, because I'm a light sleeper and I'm certain I would have heard him if he had. So from this circumstance I figure that the murderer, whoever it was, was somebody that the dog knew—maybe somebody that had worked round the place and had got to be on friendly terms with the dog."

"Did you tell this to the police?" inquired the reporter.

"Yes, I did," said the neighbor, "but they didn't seem to attach any particular importance to it."

The reporter did attach importance to it. He owned a fox terrier and he knew something of the habits of fox terriers. He knew how prone is a fox terrier to yelp when disturbed or excited. With this slender thread to guide him, the reporter, steadfastly keeping his own counsel and taking the tragedy itself for a starting point, worked backward step by step until he ferreted out the facts concerning the insurance policies. By a deft stroke, which in itself would be worth the telling as a separate narrative, he likewise found out the truth relating to the dead man's tangled personal affairs. Finally by the exercise of audacity, persistency, some diplomacy, some intimidating tactics and a great deal of deductive talent, he pieced together the clews into a fabric of circumstantial evidence which could not reasonably be disputed.

Here was a case of a reporter digging out a big story by dint of sheer ingenuity and powers of mental concentration. I recall an equally conspicuous case wherein the element of pure chance—call it luck—enabled a reporter to score a notable beat. This reporter was a green hand at the game. He had a job on an evening paper in a city in the Southwest. His beat was the city-hall beat, so-called, including the municipal offices and police and fire headquarters.

One drowsy summer afternoon, business being slack, he slipped away from his post without notifying his chief, and on a street car rode five miles up the river to the northern edge of town on a private mission having nothing at all to do with his duties. As a matter of fact, a sweetheart was the compelling motive behind his truancy. The home of the young woman's parents stood on the river bank at the end of the car line.

Just below the house one of the biggest railroad bridges in the United States was nearing completion. As the youth turned in at the yard gate he faced about to look for a minute at the great structure covered, as it was, with swarming workingmen and steam cranes and hoisting paraphernalia. At that precise moment the huge middle span collapsed, carrying with it, down to death, between fifty and seventy-five men.

The reporter dashed indoors to the telephone and flashed the word of the disaster to his office. His paper was on the street with an extra containing a thrown-together half-column summary of the horror before the staff in a rival shop two blocks away knew even that the ghastly thing had occurred. Indeed the first intimation to the opposition that a monumental news story had broken came when a popeyed circulation manager ran into the city room bearing a copy of the extra which he had snatched from a newsboy on the street below.

With the added advantage on his side of having been an eyewitness, the truant reporter poured additional details over the wire into his own shop in so steady a stream that long before any other reporter for his paper or the opposition paper reached the spot his first bulletins had been amplified into a two-column spread.

Toward dusk, having issued the final edition for the day, the city editor, through the telephone, started to congratulate him upon his coup. And then for the first time, understanding having suddenly come to him, the city editor broke off his commendatory speech to demand, "But say, look here! How the hell did you come to be away up yonder at the Point at three o'clock this afternoon, five miles from where you belong?"

With practice a reporter acquires curious coupled senses of detachment from and attachment to details. Let me illustrate: While off duty, a seasoned reporter visits, let us say, some place he has not seen before. except that his natural processes of observation are perhaps trained to a higher state of development than are those of the average layman, he views the scene with a casual eye, chambering no special impressions but taking in only the general broad outlines of the picture. It is as though he had put his reporter's bump to sleep. But let him be sent to the spot with orders to get a descriptive story and at once his vision becomes so sharpened that the salient bits of local color automatically are recorded and mentally card-indexed for use in the story he means to write.

Under another given set of circumstances the power to exercise this dual faculty is even more paradoxically exemplified. Watch a group of veteran sport writers in the press stand at a baseball game. Seemingly they pay but small heed to the game. They are chatting among themselves. Only occasionally does one of them jot down on a folded scrap of paper a word or a cabalistic cipher. But make no mistake. Not a single essential point of the game is escaping them. That night, merely by reference to a few fragmentary notes and to a copy of the box score, each one of them is able to re-create a brain photograph of every important play that occurred during the full nine innings. It is as though one lobe of his brain had been educated to follow the progress of the play while the other lobe had been left free for the discussion of unrelated matters with his mates; and that, in a way of speaking, is exactly what has happened.

There is a popular fiction to the effect that reporters delight in exaggeration. In the minds of some folk this notion goes even farther. They believe that the most valued reporters necessarily are those who are the greatest fakers. As a matter of fact, reporters who attain to distinction and to lasting reputations in their profession are the reporters who, regardless of natural impulses, cultivate the difficult art of repression and simultaneously develop an adaptability for underestimation in literary expression rather than for overestimation.

Nearly every great news event, and certainly every great crime event, is made up of two chapters running roughly in parallel lines. One of these chapters—or perhaps it would be more proper to call it a serial, since it develops from day to day as developments multiply—is the account which the public reads in print. The other is the inside story, which, for reasons of expediency or because of the danger of libel suits, or oftener still because of respect for public morals and public ethics, or sometimes because of a genuine desire to protect some innocent person from humiliation or suffering, is never printed. And this, too, despite the fact that nine times out of ten, were it printed, it would create a bigger stir than those details which go into the columns.

When one newspaper man asks another newspaper man what the inside story of such-and-such a case is he means that for his own information he desires to hear a frequently scandalous and startling budget of minutiæ which has been withheld from publication altogether, but which all the same is common gossip within the sanctity of every city room in town. The public does not appreciate, I am sure, how common is this practice; certainly the public gives the papers no credit for it.

Reverting for the moment to the personal, I fetch up out of my own experiences as an active newspaper worker memories of two occasions when by printing all that I had been told, instead of merely of a part of what I had been told, I might have scored rather impressively.

In the earlier stages of the great war, back yonder in the fall of 1914, I, serving as correspondent for *The Saturday Evening Post,* was with the German Army in Southern Belgium and Northern France.

At that time, in the official German communiqués, the Crown Prince was being credited with victory after victory. I had never seen the Crown Prince, but I had seen pictures of him, and I doubted—as did many another—whether to his military genius and strategic gifts were due the successes which the forces ostensibly under his command had been scoring in the invasion and the occupation of Allied territory. Along about this time I reached a basis of social understanding with an officer of medium rank who nevertheless stood high in the councils of the imperial general staff.

One evening at a captured château in France there was a dinner. The food was not especially plentiful, but for all who cared to drink it a gushing abundance of confiscated wine had been provided. Possibly my friend of the staff took more champagne than was good for him. At any rate his tongue loosened as the fizzy stuff warmed his brain. By someone at the table mention was made of the Crown Prince, the speaker sinking his voice to that tone of reverence which all German soldiers of high or low degree employed those times when naming any member of the royal family.

Turning to my acquaintance, the staff officer, who sat next to me, I said: "Tell me, Von Blank, is it really true the Crown Prince is personally responsible for the brilliant things with which your war office and your intelligence department credit him?"

He stared at me a moment out of those slate-blue Prussian eyes of his, and then with just the faint ghost of a smile twitching at the corners of his mouth under the spiky mustache he said to me: "My friend, listen! I am telling you this only because you are my friend. All true Germans love and admire the Crown Prince. Some day

he will succeed his illustrious father upon
the throne of the Vaterland, and from our
cradles we are taught to give obedience
and devotion to those whom we expect shall
rule over us. Besides, the Crown Prince
is naturally quick-witted, and he is a soldier by profession. But"—and here for just
a moment he paused, while his smile broadened—"but we have in our army, as commanders, men who are older than he both in
years and in the science of warfare.

"Now then the situation is this: On the
evening before an extensive movement is
expected, when all the plans have been
made, the Crown Prince is escorted to his
headquarters, which probably are some distance in the rear of the battle lines, and
there he is made comfortable and happy,
and there he remains the next day while the
fighting is progressing. You understand of
course that it never would do to permit the
heir to the throne to expose himself to the
dangers of an engagement. So!

"He stays where he is, quite serene until
near nightfall, let us say, when the fighting
is over. Then if all has gone well with our

gallant troops his generals accompany him to the Front and to him they say: 'Behold, Highness, what you have this day accomplished!' And he says: 'So! I then have done this? It is well. See to it that I do as well again to-morrow.' And then he returns to his château, and on to-morrow, *Gott* willing, it is as he has willed."

Now just at this particular time it would have interested the whole world to learn on the word of a German officer in position to know the facts that the Crown Prince was bedded down miles away from the scenes of his supposed victories. Moreover, no spoken pledge of secrecy had been exacted from me by my wine-bibbing companion when he told me this. Still there was an implied confidence in the relations existing between us. I take no particular credit to myself that I refrained from including in my dispatches the substance of what he told me; that indeed I did not so much as hint at it. I was governed merely by a sense of reportorial proprieties which had been implanted through years and years of training.

Until he read these lines in manuscript the editor of *The Saturday Evening Post* did not know that in 1914 I was in position, had I so chosen, to puncture the Crown Prince's lovely little red balloon. But having himself been a newspaper reporter once upon a time, the editor fully understood and appreciated the motives which guided me in my forbearance when the provocation to divulge the information was very strong. I feel that I can divulge it now without violation of my professional code, because there isn't any Crown Prince any more, but only a foxy-faced refugee; and the fighting force he professed to lead in 1914 is but a phalanx of ghosts, a thing formless and void.

The other personal illustration I have in mind bears upon an interview had by me with Lord Kitchener, then the head of the British War Office, which was printed in *The Saturday Evening Post* in December, 1914. It was stated at the time—not by me and not by that publication, but by sundry persons—that this was the only interview granted by Lord Kitchener to a newspaper

man in the whole of his life. As a matter
of fact, this statement was incorrect. In the
South African campaign against the Boers
Kitchener more than once made direct
statements for publication to British correspondents. But it is true that the interview I secured from him was the only one
given by him during the great World War.

Kitchener is dead and could not speak
for himself even were he so minded. To
some it may seem as though I, swollen with
a sense of my own self-importance, were
digging moldy bones out of an ancient
grave when I undertake to revive the memory of this particular incident. But for
apter illustration of the point I have been
trying to make—namely, that an experienced reporter ofttimes withholds better
stuff than he prints—I crave leave briefly
to narrate certain circumstances which
have never been printed.

Less than two weeks out of the German
front lines, I landed in London in the late
fall of 1914. I was one of three correspondents who had been vouchsafed an opportunity to accompany the invading columns

across one corner of Belgium and on into France. Naturally every Englishman with whom I came in contact was interested in having me sketch for him my impressions of the Germans as individuals and as units of a great fighting machine.

One day, in company with Doctor Jameson, the Transvaal raider, and a fellow correspondent who had been my traveling mate while we trooped with the Teutons, I was a luncheon guest at the town house of Lord Northcliffe, whom I regarded then and still regard as the greatest journalist of the English-speaking daily press. It was inevitable that the table conversation largely should deal with the things we two had seen and heard and felt while campaigning with the enemy's forces.

Early next morning a ring on the telephone lifted me out of bed at the Hotel Savoy. Over the wire a voice said: "This is Lord Northcliffe's secretary speaking. Lord Northcliffe wishes to know whether you would care to see Lord Kitchener today."

The phraseology confused me as to the

real intent of the message. I knew Lord Kitchener's reputation for confirmed reticence. I knew he was supposed never to receive personally any newspaper men. Taken by surprise as I was, I jumped at the conclusion that what Lord Northcliffe's invitation meant was that I might have opportunity, if I so desired, not to meet Lord Kitchener but merely to be at some advantageous point for seeing and for studying at close range perhaps the sphinxlike figure whose very silence had made of him a popular myth and a current superstition and who at that moment bulked so great in the eye of creation.

So I replied: "Well, I'm obliged to Lord Northcliffe, but I'm not particularly interested in seeing Lord Kitchener merely for the sake of seeing him."

Over the wire I caught an echo of the secretary's gasp of astonishment. He went on to explain: "What I mean to say is that if you care to have an audience with Lord Kitchener, Lord Northcliffe desires you to know that the matter already has been practically arranged by him. It is Lord

Northcliffe's idea that Lord Kitchener might be interested in hearing some of the things which you told Lord Northcliffe yesterday, and that you might be interested in getting some of Lord Kitchener's views."

That was different. I hastened to accept the invitation with thanks. I was told that if I would be at a certain wing in the War Office at ten o'clock I promptly would be admitted to Lord Kitchener's presence.

At ten o'clock I was there, and I spent substantially forty minutes in Lord Kitchener's company. As I stated in the article which I subsequently wrote and which was published in the *Saturday Evening Post,* Lord Kitchener put to me probably two questions for every one question I put to him. He prefaced his inquiry by telling me that if in his zeal to serve his own country he chanced to ask me something which I —in view of the fact that I had been a guest, so to speak, of the German Army—felt in honor bound not to divulge, he would not take it amiss should I decline point-blank to answer. It was on this basis of understanding that the dialogue proceeded.

On the following day, being again Lord Northcliffe's guest, I told him in detail what Lord Kitchener had told me, and I asked him whether in his opinion, he having been responsible for the meeting, and having, I take it, vouched for me to Lord Kitchener, I was justified in writing for publication in America the gist and the substance and—so far as a well-trained memory would permit—the language used by Kitchener. In effect his reply was as follows:

"To my way of thinking, there could be no impropriety in your doing that very thing. I know some of the views you have just given in quotation are substantially the same views Lord Kitchener has expressed, and some of the phraseology you have just attributed to him seems to me characteristic of his modes of thought and expression. Moreover, Lord Kitchener undoubtedly understands and appreciates that I did not bring about this meeting between you merely for social purposes. He knows, too, of course what your profession is. For his purposes he naturally wished to get something from you. For your purposes you are, I think, absolutely justified in getting a return in value from him."

When I reached America a fortnight later I wrote an honest and painstaking and, I am sure, an absolutely accurate account of the call upon Lord Kitchener. I had not taken any notes while I was with him, but almost immediately upon leaving his offices I had made a careful transcript of what he had said to me. It was these memoranda which I now used for freshening my memory. I had done the same thing scores of times before when interviewing notable men in this country.

More or less liberal extracts from my article as it appeared in *The Saturday Evening Post* were cabled to England by the resident English correspondents of some eight or ten important English daily newspapers. Following a customary procedure, these cable dispatches, on reaching British shores, were taken over by the press censor, who was an arm of the War Office and a part of the British military establishment. By the censor the dispatches, as subse-

quently developed, were held for from
twelve to eighteen hours. Then without
change or elision, without the striking out
of a word or the insertion of a word—or at
least that is my understanding—they were
released for publication in morning papers
through the British Isles.

Late that afternoon, after evening papers
all over Great Britain had had full opportunity to lift and to publish these dispatches
as reprints, some unnamed functionary in
the War Office issued a statement to the
effect that certain of the utterances attributed by me to Lord Kitchener were in
large measure imaginary, and that though
Lord Kitchener had seen me for a few minutes on a certain date, he had not given me
a special interview.

Not until nearly three weeks later, when
the editor of *The Saturday Evening Post*
received from a clipping bureau in England
a compilation of comments by British newspapers upon the controversy, did I or my
employers know the circumstances govern-
ing the handling of the cable dispatches on
the other side of the ocean. And likewise

not until then did we know *The London Times* had stated editorially that if my version of Lord Kitchener's remarks was willfully or unintentionally false, that if in what I had set down as purporting to be the essence of his language I had distorted his words or given a misleading or incorrect twist to his meanings, it devolved upon the press censor, as a part of the War Office, to suppress the dispatches outright upon their arrival instead of permitting them to attain a wide circulation before issuing the denial of authenticity. In other words, the time to scotch a lie is when it is young rather than after it has attained lusty proportions and has spawned a whole breed of lesser lies and contradictions and repudiations and protestations.

Now, then, by this somewhat roundabout route I come to the point I have been seeking to make. In the course of his conversation with me Lord Kitchener uttered two things which, had I written them—and I might very well have done so, since he had no way of stopping me—would have given to the printed interview an interest greater

than it had.　Speaking of his chief military
opponent, Von Kluck, and with particular
reference to the latter's conduct of the advance which had been checked at the
Marne, he said Von Kluck had made an ass
of himself.　These were his exact words.
A few minutes later, in referring to the
treatment of Belgian noncombatants by the
Germans, he said the conduct of the Germans, who called themselves a civilized
race, was comparable to the conduct of the
savages against whom he had fought years
before in his Khartum campaign.

Taking counsel with myself, I elected to
leave out of my manuscript these two significant utterances.　With regard to the first
I believed that if Lord Kitchener had had
opportunity—which he did not—to read the
draft of my interview he would on second
thought have stricken out his remark regarding General Von Kluck.　Accordingly,
then, of my own volition I excluded it from
the quoted matter.

With regard to the second statement I
had the fear in my mind that the Germans,
reading where Kitchener had likened their

behavior to the behavior of a horde of un-
disciplined and fanatical Africans, might
profess to believe Kitchener had intent to
serve wounded Germans who fell into his
hands after the same summary fashion of
extinction in which he was popularly supposed to have served wounded barbarians
in the Sudan and that, acting on this infer-
ence, the Germans for their part might find
alleged justification for retaliating upon
wounded British captives.

Privately I satisfied my own conscience.
Publicly I had to face the imputation that
I had misquoted one of the most prominent
men alive at that time. To me, though, the
conviction that professionally and personally I had kept the faith more than balanced
the journalistic stigma. At the same time I
may as well confess that ever since the thing
happened I have been waiting suitable opportunity and occasion for setting forth
my version of my side of the dispute between that anonymous statement maker of
the British War Office and myself.

Newspapers are supposed to be published
mainly for the benefit of their readers. So

far as the reporter is concerned he is working all the time for the glory of the paper, which means incidentally his own glory, with an eye single to the main impression which will be created in the minds of those who read what he has helped to fashion. Of editors as a class this is not so true. Mind you, I speak of them as a class, and not with regard to the exceptions of a somewhat common rule.

Many editors edit newspapers with a view to the effect upon other editors of other papers. I know sundry members of my craft will take issue with me in this assertion, but nevertheless I maintain that I am not far wrong. The trouble, I think, is that editors, being indoor creatures and chained up close to the thing they serve, lose in a measure the sense of perspective and sometimes the almost infallible sense of news values which very possibly distinguished them when they were reporters and were not closely attached to the shop, but on the other hand ranged afield, coming daily in direct contact with outside causes and outside influences.

When I say an editor may edit his paper for the sake of the reactions upon his brother editor across the road I mean just this: In his mind a beat, as they call it, in New York and Chicago, or a scoop, as they call it in most other cities, acquires its chief attraction through the fact that it will fill with envy the soul of some outdistanced or outwitted rival. Accordingly he very frequently will play up on the front page a piece of news which happens to be exclusive, without regard to its actual attractions for the public.

In my own case it was necessary for me to divorce myself from work on the daily press before I came to perceive that the so-called exclusive nearly always has very much less interest for the reader than it has for the men who feature it in the make-up. The reader, I am sure, judges a paper and favors it or does not favor it, as the case may be, on its merits and its lack of merits in the essentials of its typographical appearance, its literary style and its customary tone in the treatment of publishable events and public issues rather than because three weeks ago it was first upon the street by a margin of half an hour with the verdict in a murder trial, or because to-morrow it may be the only paper in town to announce the filing of a sensational divorce suit.

Inside the shops these coups are deemed precious as rare jewels. Over them there is much boasting and for them special awards are given. Outside, barring only Newspaper Row, they promptly are forgotten. Indeed I am certain that except among newspaper men they generally go unnoticed. To my way of thinking, the ideal news editor would be one who handled his news according to his own tastes without ever seeing contemporary sheets. Only, of course, as the yokel said when he saw the giraffe, "There ain't no such animal!"

By reason of his state of semidetachment from the outer world and his state of complete attachment to the job he holds, your average editor often develops a perverted idea of the importance, from a news standpoint of view, of whatsoever may transpire which directly affects the paper itself. The owner of a big metropolitan daily dies. To

the public at large the news of his death and
the details of the life he has lived mean just
as much as similar tidings regarding any
man equally conspicuous in any other calling—mean exactly so much and no more.
But do the editors of the paper which he
owned think so? And do they in the columns over which they preside govern themselves accordingly? Not so that you could
notice it.

In 1918, when Mr. James Gordon Ben-
net died, I was in Paris. On the day following the Paris edition of *The New York
Herald* devoted the greater part of its reading space to his death. This perhaps was
as it should be. Mr. Bennett was the founder of the Paris edition of *The Herald* and
its chief proprietor, just as his father before him had been the founder and the main
proprietor of the parent sheet in New York;
and he had been an outstanding figure in
the journalism of his generation and a person of consequence in many spheres of activity. But day after day, stretching on
into weeks, the Paris *Herald* reprinted commendatory editorials from big and little and

medium-sized papers in America and in Europe, all dealing with the life, death and works of Mr. Bennett. It continued to print them even though some of them were weeks old before they reached France; continued to print them despite the fact that the crisis of the Great War was reaching its culmination and that every word about the progress of the supreme battle then raging a few miles to the north of Paris was of enormous interest to every English-speaking person within the scope of the paper's Continental circulation. The thing came to be a joke among the correspondents.

Across the breakfast table one man would say to another, "What's in the *Herald* this morning?" And the second would reply, "Well, I see by the paper that Mr. Bennett is still dead."

There is record of at least one instance where vanity, and not modesty, led a paper to the opposite extreme. On October 17, 1897, Charles A. Dana died after having ruled over the destinies of *The New York Sun* for thirty years. What happened is told in Mr. Frank M. O'Brien's most interesting book, "The Story of The Sun." This is what Mr. O'Brien has written:

"A few years before, on observing an obituary paragraph which Mr. Dana had written about some noted man, John Swinton asked his chief how much space he—Swinton—would get when his time came.

"'For you, John, two sticks,' said Mr. Dana. Turning to Mr. Mitchell, then his chief editorial writer, he added. 'For me, two lines.'

"On the morning after Mr. Dana's death every newspaper but one in New York printed columns about the career of the dean of American journalism. *The Sun* printed only ten words, and these were carried at the head of the first editorial column without a heading:

"'Charles Anderson Dana, editor of *The Sun,* died yesterday afternoon.'"

As I said just now, I do not think this was modesty. To my mind it was an exhibition of vanity masking itself as modesty. But whether we credit it to modesty or to vanity, the outstanding fact is that an injustice was done to the readers of *The Sun*. Mr. Dana was one of the biggest men of his time, but no man is too big for an obituary. The readers of *The Sun* were as fully entitled to an adequate account of his life and to a presentation of the facts of his last illness

and his death and the plans for his funeral
as were the readers of any paper. In other
words, I thing *The Sun* should have treated
the death of Mr. Dana, not as *The Herald*
subsequently treated the death of Mr. Bennett, but substantially as *The Herald* probably treated the death of Mr. Dana; that is
to say, with dignity and respect and a rea-
sonable and balanced fullness as to detail.
To my way of thinking, this is the one glaring journalistic mistake which may be
charged to the old *Sun,* which then, when
Mr. Dana died, and for years thereafter
was, in the opinion of a majority of newspaper men, the best morning paper that
ever was printed anywhere.

It is a part of the penalty which most
reporters pay for the jealous taskmistress
they serve with an entire devotion that
they uniformly must sink their own personalities in the personalities of the papers on
which they are employed. I am not speaking of the conspicuous one-tenth—the special writers who sign their names to what
they write and the likes of them. I am
speaking of the submerged nine-tenths, the

ordinary reporters who run their legs off
and risk their lives and their limbs to get the
news, knowing all the while that oftener
than not other men will write the stories
and get the main credit if the stories are
well written.

For years now newspapers all over
America have been carrying articles to
prove how ill paid are teachers and preach-
ers and clerks and bookkeepers and the
white-collared groups generally. The figures to bolster up these arraignments are
collected and compiled and in many in-
stances written out by reporters and sub-
editors, who, considering all that they must
know and all that they must give to their
jobs, are more shamefully underpaid than
any of the classes upon whom they shower
a meed of sympathy and for whom they demand a proper justice in the matter of pay
envelopes. Outside of New York, Chicago,
Philadelphia, Boston and perhaps one or
two other cities—possibly St. Louis and San
Francisco should be added to the list—the
rank and file of city-room staffs, the lads in
the trenches and the kids behind the guns,

receive less wages in proportion to the labor they do and the sacrifices they make and the physical and mental exertions they undergo than do school-teachers or dry-goods clerks.

But do you find any passionate and excited articles in the daily newspapers calling for better pay for newspaper men? You do not! In the first place it doesn't seem to occur to the newspaper man that he should include himself along with the rest of the undersalaried industrials. In the second place, if he had the temerity to dare to do it, it wouldn't be printed.

In 1920 at the height of the post-war inflation in wages and prices, a suburban correspondent of a paper which is published in a large city near by dropped into a savings bank in the town where he lived. It is assumed that his call was purely social in its nature. Being a reporter, he naturally wouldn't have any money to deposit. And being a reporter, he naturally couldn't expect to be able to borrow any money from the bank. The teller was a friend of his —one of his occasional sources of news.

"See yonder?" said the teller, pointing

to an overalled alien of a Slavic aspect who languidly was mopping off a plate glass at the front of the establishment. "Well, every time I look at that Hunkie I get mad. I've been with this bank for going on fifteen years now. He's been working for it for about two months. I have to wear good clothes and clean linen and keep my finger nails clean and my hair cut and my face shaved. I have to give bond for my honesty and I am responsible for the handling of thousands of dollars every week. He doesn't have to do any of those things. I sometimes work twelve or even sixteen hours a day. He never works more than eight hours in a day. He's unskilled and I'm skilled. But he's organized and I'm not. I don't know whether there's a union of window washers in this town, but I know there's a combine of them strong enough to do a lot of dictating. And so the consequence is that I draw thirty-five dollars a week from this bank and he draws forty-two."

Knowing that the recital of the teller's grievance would make a human-interest story, the reporter went away and wrote a little piece about it and sent it in and his paper next morning printed it. No names were given, of course, but the townsfolk readily identified the bank in question, inasmuch as it happened to be the only savings bank in the town. One result was that the teller came very near to losing his job, and the other result was that the window washer struck for a three-dollar-a-week-increase—and got it—because publication of the yarn led to the discovery on his part that divers window washers in the same neighborhood were getting forty-five dollars a week instead of forty-two.

But the real joke didn't come out. The reporter, who had to apply as much intelligence and ability and technical knowledge to his job as the paying teller applied to his, and who had to keep longer hours than the window washer kept, was getting ten dollars a week less than the paying teller got and twenty dollars less than the window cleaner got after the story appeared.

CHAPTER FIVE

"I Admit I Am a Good Reporter"

CHAPTER V

"I Admit I Am a Good Reporter"

IF anybody claims I am an authentic
humorist I can show him a scrap-book
full of clippings, signed by expert book
reviewers, to prove the contrary. If anybody thinks me a rising young short-story
writer—that is to say, young for my age,
which is the only way a body ever is young
or ever is old, either, for that matter—I repeat, if anybody chooses to regard me as one
giving promise as a short-story writer, I can
cure the obsession by producing another
volume of criticisms done by men and wom-
en who freely concede that they know all
there is to know about the short-story-writ-
ing game and who are equally frank and
aboveboard in telling me what I do not
know about it. But if anybody says I am
not a good reporter, I'll bet him a million
dollars he is a liar.

I am a good reporter, and I admit it and I can prove it and I am proud of it. I know how to go out and get a news story and how to assemble the stuff afterward. I know how to play on a news story as though it were a concertina or a crush hat; which is to say I know how to stretch a small story out to the length of a column, and by the same token how to pack down a big story into the compass of a paragraph.

I can gather my facts in the midst of noise and excitement, and if needs be I can write them down in the midst of more noise and more excitement. With one lobe of my brain I can think of the story I am writing and with the other lobe of my brain I can be watching the clock and keeping tally of the narrowing margin of minutes between now and press time.

I can interview a man and listen to him while he airs his views for half an hour or an hour and never take out my pencil except to scribble down dates or proper names. And then I can go back to the shop and put on paper the sense of what he said in the sequence in which he said it and, generally speaking, I can reproduce from memory the language he used in saying it.

If the city editor tells me to write two hundred words about something, I can write for him two hundred words. I do not need to count them off or measure them up. When I have done the stint and pulled the sheet of copy paper out of my typewriter and sent it over to his desk, I am willing to risk any sum within reason that it will run within ten words of two hundred words. There is no trick about it; a subconscious something, an instinct born of long training, mechanically warns me when I have done two hundred words, or five hundred or a thousand—not five hundred or a thousand, approximately, but almost literally that number.

My weakest point is a tendency to overwrite, to over-elaborate, a story which interests me personally. (Perhaps I am overwriting now.) My strongest point is a sense of news values; I suppose you might call it an inherent sense, for it seems to me that I have had it ever since the beginning of my apprenticeship. My heaviest liability

in the line of outstanding reportorial shortcomings is an almost complete absence of
the deductive quality, wherefore effects appeal to me rather than causes. As an ana-
lyst I would never shine unless it were with
that same shininess which we associate with
a brass dime. Many reporters are clever
detectives; but as a detective on piece work
I would starve to death.

On the other hand, my best assets are
an excellent memory and an ability, first,
mentally to photograph a scene or a person,
and then to stow the picture away in a sort
of filing system inside my head, where it
stays properly catalogued and indexed
against the time when I want to take it out
and use it. In fine and in short, I am a
good reporter, and if you don't believe I am
—why, I am, that's all.

I am not a born reporter; I never saw
one. I have known men who as cubs started
with a natural aptitude for the trade, and
who therefore learned it rapidly and well.
I have seen men who had less aptitude for
it, and who therefore learned it slowly and
laboriously. I have seen men who had no

aptitude at all for it, and they never became star reporters, no matter how hard they tried. These men might have made good railroad presidents or good railroad switchmen, might have written essays or verses or novels or life insurance or underwear advertisements. But they could not handle news stories because they lacked what we call a nose for news, which means an appreciation of news values.

Reporting, like any other specialized work, is a trade to be learned, not one to be born with. And I learned mine. I acquired it by experience, by making the same mistake so often that, after a while, I learned not to make it quite so often At the time this goes into print I am nearing my forty-sixth birthday. I have been doing reporting since I was half past sixteen; which means that for thirty years, nearly, I have been reporting for daily papers, weekly papers, trade papers, and Sunday papers; for syndicates, press associations, periodicals and magazines.

Sometimes in my veteran's vanity I figure that I know the reporting game from

Dan to Beersheba. Then I read a story by Sam Blythe or Martin Green or Frank O'Malley or Damon Runyon, and I realize that I still have a good deal to learn about this lifetime trade of mine.

I have known men who qualified in the eyes of city editors as good reporters merely because they were good writers. This in my opinion was a mistake. The real test of a real reporter is not so much his ability to write as it is his ability to get the news, and to do that he must know news by the very smell of it, and never for one moment be content to take that which somebody else may think is the news.

In this most essential part of his calling every seasoned reporter has his own method of getting the desired result. One of the best reporters I know is a man who works by devious and roundabout methods. He has a natural flair for intrigue. He figures that the world is in a conspiracy to throw him off the right track, and he conspires with himself to circumvent the forces which, he thinks, are plotting against him. He generally succeeds, too, having a nimbler mind than the average one against which he pits his wits.

He is not far wrong in his original premise, either. The fabled old gentleman of Virginia who made a fortune by minding his own business was not a newspaper man. I am sure of that. Because a newspaper man's business is other people's business. For it is just that—"other people's business" —which provides the news that the world at large wants to read. Excluding the pleasant affairs of everyday life and the heroic events there is scarcely an imaginable happening the real facts of which it is not someone's private or personal interest to keep out of print.

Ninety-nine times out of a hundred printting the news means hurting some individual in feelings, prestige or purse; it means telling something which someone would much rather were never told. It follows that, in every news story involving what is called human interest, the reporter may be quite sure that at some point in his investigation of the circumstances he will encounter an individual or a group of individuals who by every means in their power will endeavor to hide from him certain salient and, from his viewpoint, desirable details.

This compatriot of mine whom I mentioned in a preceding paragraph goes on the broad general principle that practically the entire planet is in a plot to defeat his ends, which are the digging out of the truth, the whole truth, and nothing but the truth.

Not that a newspaper always prints the truth after it gets it. A regard for public morals or for the common ethics of life may demand that some of the facts either be hinted at or suppressed altogether. Then what is not printed becomes the "inside story," a thing to which I already have referred in a preceding chapter of this book.

When one newspaper man asks another newspaper man what the inside story of a certain matter is, he means he wants to know those hidden details which the general public probably will never know—the written laws of libel and the unwritten laws of common decency being what they are —but which, heard in private, will give to the initiated a clearer idea of the affair than he could get from the printed column. Hence, "inside story." But an editor wants to have all the details in his possession, whether or not he means to exploit them. And it is the business of the reporter to get them for him.

A good detective, I take it, is an honest man who can think like a thief; who mentally can put himself inside the skin of a criminal and figure out just what, under a given or a presumed set of circumstances, a criminal would do. This friend of mine would make an admirable detective. He begins by deciding what he himself would do or say were he in the position of the person who, he believes, is trying to protect himself or someone else from the consequences of a misdeed, or a mistake, as the case may be.

This done, he takes steps to entrap his chosen quarry into making the desired admissions. He may gain his point by winning the person's confidence. He may achieve it by a bluff or by bullying tactics.

He may pose as a police officer, or as a

coroner's physician, or as a sympathizing friend of a friend of the suspect. He may assume any one of a dozen rôles, for in addition to being a wonderful judge of human nature he is a good actor.

Now my method almost invariably has been the exact opposite of this. Having no instinct for intrigue and mighty little of the deductive quality in my make-up, I generally have had recourse to the direct approach, the frontal attack, as you might say. My plan has been to go straight to the person who, I believed, could furnish me with the information I needed and in so many words to ask that person for that information. If he turned me down I was done with that person. But it very often happened that he did not turn me down. In fact my system has successfully operated so often that I am convinced it is, for me at least, the best possible system.

I recall two sundry incidents in point. Here is one of them: Some years ago there was a Tenderloin murder of a spectacular sort. One of the by-products of that murder was the disclosure of a scandal affecting a branch of the police department. Pretty soon, what with the uncovering of a system of wholesale grafting and official connivance at crime, the side issue became of more importance for purposes of newspaper publicity than the original crime. In connection with this corruption, a promising young detective, a member of the so-called Vice Squad, was indicted under the criminal code. In the court-room, while being arraigned for a preliminary hearing, he tried to kill himself with his own revolver.

A little later he was sentenced to state's prison. Because it was shown that before temptation came to him he had been a straightforward and zealous officer, and because, before he went on the force, he had been an honor man of the fire department with a record for conspicuous gallantry, the judge showed him as much mercy as possible. His term of imprisonment was to be a short one.

In New York the average "sensation" rarely lasts for the proverbial nine days. Something more timely or more exciting speedily crowds it off the front page. But this particular sensation lived longer than some do by reason of its day-to-day developments. After it had run its course and languished, my city editor—and a mighty smart one he was—evolved a theory that the biggest part of the story had never yet come to light. He believed that if we could get at the real bowels of this scandal we would be able to show that the ramifications of the intrigue, which bound certain members of the police department to certain ignoble notables of the underworld, went deeper into the roots of high-up officialdom than had been suspected. He scented that thing so dear to the souls of city editors— an "exclusive exposé." He detailed me to work on this hypothesis.

"Use your own judgment," he said. "I don't know how you'll get this story; but I'm satisfied the story is there. Now go to it."

Here is what I did: I caught a Centre Street car for Park Row, rode up to the Tombs, and sent my card to the young ex-police detective in his cell. A turnkey brought him down-stairs. If ever I saw a brokenhearted man in my life, here was one. On the following morning he would be taken, handcuffed, up the river. Going, he would leave behind him the broken shards of what had been a promising career. Coming back again, when he had served his time, he would face the prospect of starting life all over again, with a black mark against his name.

Until now he had steadily refused to make any confession involving others. In the parlance of the System "he had been caught with the goods, so he would take his medicine and keep his face shut." At least, so those who had reason to wish him to stay silent had figured it out. It was my idea, though, that the thought that next day Sing Sing's doors would be opening for him might possibly make him change his mind.

With no attempt at deceit, without making any promise to him of influence to be exerted in his behalf, but in plain, straightforward language, I told him the nature of my assignment and asked his help in getting the story. Without a moment's hesitation he answered:

"I'm glad you came. I've been thinking things over here lately—I've had time to do a lot of thinking. I'm not taking any high moral ground, but I honestly believe that maybe, by telling the inside of the rotten game that I got tangled up in, I can keep some other young cop who started out straight, like I did, from going crooked. Now then, have you got pencil and paper handy? All right! I'll start at the beginning and tell you all I know about this whole mess."

For a solid hour he talked to me. He gave me dates, names, and places. I came away freighted with startling admissions and even more startling accusations. The story I got from him, practically without any prompting on my part, would have made a town-shaking beat—but for one thing.

That night while I was grinding out the copy from the data he had given me, Harry K. Thaw, on the roof of Madison Square Garden, killed the great architect, Stanford

White! The next morning, so far as creating any public stir went, my story might just as well have been left out of print altogether.

I have in mind an even more illuminating example to show that the dead-ahead plan of going after things may pay desirable dividends. This story was of more than local importance, even more than national importance. It was the biggest story the world has known since the Crucifixion.

In the early autumn of 1914, three of us landed in the German border city of Aix la Chapelle. We had been brought there as prisoners from southern Belgium by the Germans. With the aid of the American consul at Aix and through the good offices of Ambassador Gerard, we convinced the agents of the Imperial Government that we were neither spies nor Britishers posing as Americans, but were what we claimed to be, properly-accredited correspondents from a then neutral country. But although we no longer were dogged by German secret service men, we were cooped up in that town as effectually as though we had been under lock and key.

Within a fortnight word reached us—no matter how—that the German military rulers were about to relax the rule against permitting correspondents to travel with their armies of invasion. They were going to permit one chosen group of writers from neutral nations to make a trip along the western front. At the same time we were informed that the chances for our party of three to be included in this excursion were about one in a thousand.

We were many miles from Berlin, with no means of getting there. We had been in custody and still were under suspicion. There were resident correspondents in Berlin who knew the heads of the German Government. Some of these men had been stationed in Berlin for years. It was natural to suppose that to them would come first the coveted opportunity of going to the front.

Nevertheless, we promptly made application through official channels for the great privilege. So doing, we used the wires and the mails. In return we received polite but ambiguous messages from various chancellories.

We grew more and more desperate. Every day the face of war was shifting; any hour the selected correspondents might be starting under military escort for the battle lines; any hour after that the rule of absolute exclusion for our kind might be revived.

One afternoon we three went to the Kaiser's unofficial civilian representative in Aix la Chapelle, a wealthy German manufacturer who had rendered various friendly services to us. We told him we meant to write a personal letter to the Emperor asking that we three be allowed forthwith to visit the imperial forces in the field, and we requested his valuable offices in expediting the transmission of this letter to High Headquarters, wherever High Headquarters might be.

Well, when he had rallied somewhat he told us in strained and startled tones that what we desired was impossible, preposterous, unheard of. It just naturally wasn't done, and that was all there was to it.

"Why," he said, "you gentlemen do not know the court etiquette in such matters as these; you do not even know the proper language in which to address His Majesty."

"Quite right," the spokesman for our trio answered. "And because we do not know these things we are not going to make the mistake of trying to employ them in this experiment. You have told us before now that your emperor is a great business man. Well, if he is, then a good, smart, business letter should appeal to him. And that is exactly what we mean to write—a business letter. He says he wants the American people to know something authentic about the conduct of his troops. Through the magazine which one of us serves and through the newspapers which the other two represent we are in a position to reach the widest possible circulation in America. We're going to tell him so, in a letter. And now the question is, will you undertake to start that letter forward by wire through the proper channels after we write it?"

This second shock to his Prussian sensibilities seemed almost as severe as the first one had been. Having somewhat recovered, he warned us that the entire machinery of officialdom would stand as a stone wall between us and the impiety we contemplated.

"Why, gentlemen," he protested, "the first military censor into whose hands your letter came would probably stop it then and there! By personal influence I might possibly get your remarkable communication as far as Berlin. I am quite sure it would never get any farther than that."

"Never mind that," we said; "we're committed to the attempt. We only want to be sure of your help up to the limit of your powers."

Before we left him we had worn down his powers of resistance. He quit expostulating, quit arguing in opposition to our deluded scheme; he gave his reluctant consent to aid us, but disclaimed any responsibility for the possible consequences of our madness.

So we went away and in conference

drafted our letter—a plain business letter setting forth a plain business proposition; a letter not too formal, and yet, I trust, not too chatty. When it had been properly translated into German we took it back to our unhappy legate.

On reading it he suffered Shock III. Nevertheless, being a man of his word, he took it and prepared to start it upon its way. He then bade us good night in a voice which seemed to indicate he did not expect to see us soon again, if at all. His attitude was one of unspoken sympathy for three comparatively harmless lunatics who shortly would vanish out of his life forevermore.

We sat down to wait. We waited three days. On the morning of the fourth day came a gorgeous military figure, wrapped in a magnificent long gray coat, with medals on his chest and the badges of a staff colonel on his uniform. He bore to us an imposing parchment document, heavy with seals and ribbons, on which, in German script, was a statement, a proclamation, informing all whom it might concern

—and, as it turned out, it seemed deeply to concern everybody in the German army, from field marshals down, who had the inestimable privilege of reading it—that under escort of a designated officer, we three, naming us, might go pretty much where we pleased in and about the German battle lines, might have the exclusive use of a military automobile of size sufficient for our needs, might make notes, carry cameras, and take photographs, might commandeer food and tires and gasolene and billets, might bear arms for our own defense— might do, in fact, almost anything we pleased so long as we observed military regulations and respected the customary restrictions. And it was signed by the Kaiser in his own fair hand.

Again the direct-approach form of campaign had scored a triumph. Howsomever, I shall not deny that once in a while in my own experience trick and device have been resorted to, but usually, though, only as a last resort when the straightforward system had completely failed.

Remember, as I said before, the world,

most of the time, is in a conspiracy to keep a newspaper man from getting that which he desires to make copy of. The wise city editor is the one who never asks how his men attain their results, providing only they do attain them. Every successful reporter keeps the faith with his fellows, and I never yet knew a successful reporter who broke faith with those who gave him information in confidence. These two things are his creed and his code and the base-boards of his ethics. But toward those who plot to deceive him, or to throw obstacles between him and his legitimate journalistic objects, he feels he is free to adopt different tactics.

For example: Four of us were the only newspaper men who saw the taking of Louvain by the Germans. Three days later, on a Saturday afternoon, when the Germans had released us from custody at Louvain, we made our way back to Brussels. The city had been in German hands then since Thursday noon and the efficiency engine was in full operation, as we discovered

Sunday morning when we set out from our hotel on some errand or other.

At the corner of the street an over-zealous under-officer arrested us, presumably on suspicion of being Englishmen, and marched us to an improvised barracks, where his superior officer questioned us, apologized to us, and freed us. But before we had walked fifty yards farther another underling nabbed us. We traveled up the street and back again to the refuge of the hotel by a process of progressive arrests.

Inside the hotel we encountered one of our compatriots who had been staying in Brussels to witness its occupation.

"How does a fellow move around this town without an escort of bayonets?" we demanded. "These guards of honor that insist on attaching themselves to us if we poke our noses outside that door yonder embarrass us."

"Oh, that's easy!" he said. "When the Germans first arrived somebody arrested us every ten feet or so. So all the American newspaper representatives who were here went in a body to see the military governor, and he gave each one of us a pass so we could move around without being nabbed by fussy sergeants and lieutenants and things."

"Where is this accommodating commandant?" we inquired.

"Right around the corner at the Hotel de Ville."

"Lead us to him."

Under our associate's guidance, to the Hotel de Ville we went. In the main hallway we met the military governor, one Major General Thaddeus von Jarotsky. In appearance and manner he was a typical Prussian, with the lynx eyes and spiny mustache of his breed. Our friend presented the four of us, and we showed our credentials and asked for passes similar to those which our confrères had secured of him.

"With pleasure," said the general, in excellent English. "But, gentlemen, I am just on the point of going to lunch. I am late for my appointment now. Besides, I have let my staff go for the afternoon. My secretaries and my clerks and my orderlies have been working night and day ever since we reached Brussels, and I have given them a few hours for rest and sleep." He considered a moment, then went on: "As I recall, one of your fraternity speaks and writes German, is it not so?"

"I am the man, General," spoke up the correspondent who had piloted us hither.

"Ach, good! Will you, sir, be good enough to make for each of these four gentlemen a pass similar to the one you carry, merely substituting their names where your own name appears. Have these passes here at two-thirty o'clock, when I shall return, and I shall then validate them."

Back to the hotel we hurried and our sponsor unlimbered his typewriter and prepared to fill the order. We, the prospective beneficiaries, clustered about him. He took his own pass out of his pocket and laid it down alongside him.

It was a sheet of paper with two typewritten lines in German on it. Translated the lines read:

"Mr. Harry So-and-so, writer for the American press, is entitled through the German lines to pass, in Brussels and its suburbs."

There was no signature, but the stamp of the Imperial Government and the stamp of the military government which the Germans had set up in Brussels were affixed to it.

I have forgotten now which one of us it was who at this juncture had the great inspiration.

"Hold on," he said, "don't start copying yet. Isn't this General von Jarotsky rather a fussy, snappy, automatic sort of person? That's the way he struck me."

"You've sized him up," said the man at the typewriter. "But what's the idea?"

"The idea is this," said the inspired one. "When you make out my pass just leave off the final words 'in Brussels and suburbs.' See? I'm going to take a big risk. If the old boy stamps my pass without reading it too closely I'll have a document in my pocket that'll take me anywhere the Germans go—unless I have the bad luck to run into somebody above the rank of a major general."

"But suppose he does read it closely?"

"Why, in that case we'll tell him that in your haste to copy our passes before eating lunch you must have made the mistake of leaving something out. We'll ask him to let us come on back here and get corrected copies made." He turned to the other three:

"How about you fellows? Are you willing to gamble, too? The worst that can happen is that we'll be tied up here, and as things stand we're just the same as prisoners, anyway. The best that may happen is that we can slip out of here and possibly follow the Germans clear to Paris —if they get that far."

By acclamation the motion carried. At two-thirty o'clock we were at the Hotel de Ville, each with his little typewritten joker in his hand. Prompt on the minute the general reappeared. Four nervous conspirators quit breathing as he took the precious slips. But the trick worked—oh, how smoothly, how beautifully it did work. Von Jarotsky barely glanced at the papers. In another minute they had been stamped and returned to us, and we were bowing ourselves out of the presence.

In five minutes more we had chartered a couple of open carriages, each drawn by a pair of crowbait horses and driven by a red-faced Fleming who would go anywhere for a price. Ten minutes later we had passed the sentry posts of the environs and were sliding through the rear lines of the main German column on our way out on the road to Waterloo, headed toward where big guns boomed constantly with a sound like distant summer thunder. And before night we were in the back eddies of a battle which future generations will list among the great battles of the world. They'll call it by the name of The Battle of Mons.

Richard Harding Davis had one of an earlier issue of passes, which bound him to the environs of the city. That was why he, following in our tracks next day, was turned back, after having a close call from being shot. But we kept going for a week; seeing skirmishes, forced marches and rear guard actions; seeing something epochal every waking hour—until we reached the border between France and Belgium, with the cannon of Maubeuge booming not nine miles away from us. I wonder sometimes how much farther we might have gone if only we had not blundered into the fourth son of the Kaiser and a whole flock of field marshals. Blundering into them was what landed us in Aix la Chapelle and led indirectly to our writing that letter to Kaiser Wilhelm.

Stickfuls

CHAPTER SIX

Big Moments of Big Trials

CHAPTER VI

Big Moments of Big Trials

EVERY big criminal trial has its big moments—when the prisoner takes the stand, when the lawyers make their summing-up speeches, when the jury brings in the verdict—but these come at spaced intervals, like the climaxes of a play, dividing the action of the trial off into separate acts. The supreme scene of all breaks, nearly always, with no warning. Often it grows out of some seemingly trivial incident, some seemingly unimportant bit of testimony. Nearly every time it comes as a surprise to one side or the other, sometimes it is a surprise to both sides. But when it does come, it comes big with importance for the man or the woman whose life is the stake in the game, and on the instant the atmosphere of the courtroom changes. The reporters hunch their shoulders above the press table and send their pencils racing across the copy paper on the hop, skip and jump. The lolling jurymen straighten in their chairs. The judge on the bench bends forward, alert and watchful. Heads among the spectators come frontward at the same angle, like an assemblage at prayer. The opposing lawyers are on their feet, one fighting to get this evidence in its entirety, the other fighting to keep it out or to blunt down its edge and cripple its force. About the ears of the two fencers, interruptions, objections, cross objections and exceptions buzz in swarms like stinging gnats. From the crowd rises a little, subdued, humming sound never heard anywhere else. And the witness on the stand is telling, in broken scraps, the story which means ruin to the accused, or his salvation. It is the Big Moment.

One of the great murder trials that took place in New York was that of Albert Wolter for the murder of Ruth Wheeler. Albert Wolter was a half-grown immigrant boy, a sinister compound of ignorance and guile. He lived in the rear tenement of the top floor of a tenement house in East

Seventy-fifth Street, with a girl called Katchen Miller. There were no high lights to Katchen Miller. She only flitted across the canvas momentarily, but it seemed to me I had never seen so dun-colored a human being in my life. Her personality, her mind, her hair, were all the same dull tint. Katchen Miller worked as a kitchen drudge for seven dollars a week in a German coffee and cakes saloon around the corner in Third Avenue, and living on her earnings this boy, Albert Wolter, took his ease. His idle hands found some particularly bad work to do.

In the Help Wanted columns of a morning paper one day Wolter read the advertisements of a shorthand and typewriting school seeking places for its graduates, and he answered three of them by mail, inviting the applicants to call. Luck saved the first two girls. One distrusted the look of the house and turned back at the door. The second went home and consulted her parents first; and her father realizing, from his knowledge of the neighborhood, that a reputable concern would hardly be doing business in a quarter tenanted almost exclusively by the poorer classes of foreigners, told his daughter to stay away from the place.

Finally, on the third day, which was Good Friday, came Ruth Wheeler, seventeen years old, a pretty, red-haired, blue-eyed girl, born in Alabama of native American parentage. Her father, a railroad engineer, had been killed in a wreck. Her mother was a refined, energetic little woman who did fine needlework. There were two older sisters, one the head of a department in a big store, and the other the confidential secretary of a publisher. Ruth, the youngest of the three, had graduated from one of the numerous stenographic schools that flourish in New York and was looking for work. Under its contract with its students, the school was bound to secure a place for her. On this Friday morning she went to the school, dressed in her best clothes, and the principal handed her a postal card signed with a rubber stamp, "A. A. Wolter, Secretary," and giving an address in East Seventy-fifth Street. For all that she had spent most of her life in a populous part of the big city, Ruth Wheeler, to use an overworked comparison, was as innocent as a child. Later, through the testimony, we were to get an intimate picture of the little household where the mother and the older sisters watched jealously over the baby, as they called her, to protect her from every smirching influence.

Ruth Wheeler took the postal card in her hand and rode on a street-car to East Seventy-fifth Street. Two women tenants in the building saw her mounting the steps to Wolter's room. One of them pointed out the way to her. She went up the steps, and she never came down.

That night, after Ruth Wheeler's elder sister had traced Ruth to Wolter's flat and had brought the police to help her search for the missing girl, Wolter and Katchen Miller fled to other lodgings. The next day he was arrested—for abduction only. On the third day one of Wolter's recent neighbors found a bundle wrapped in burlap on the fire escape outside the window of the flat lately deserted by Wolter and Katchen Miller. She called her husband, who pushed the cumbersome thing off the narrow balcony, so that it dropped into the yard four floors below. Then, having noticed something unusual about the weight and feel of it, the man went down-stairs to where the bundle lay, cast off the ropes and piano wire which held the sacking together in a roll and found what was left of little Ruth Wheeler—a headless trunk; she had been choked, beaten, dismembered with a knife and burned with fire.

I doubt if there ever was a crime that stirred New York to deeper levels. Within five days the Grand Jury, laying aside all lesser matters, had indicted Wolter for murder in the first degree. Within two weeks the Legislature at Albany had enacted a law requiring the managers of stenographic schools carefully to investigate the standing of strangers who applied to them for clerical help.

In a little more than a month Wolter was facing a jury before Judge Warren W.

Foster in the Criminal Courts Building.
In that month the assistant district attorney
in charge of the prosecution, Frank Moss,
had prepared a case that was well-nigh
faultless. Having to rely entirely upon circumstantial evidence for convicting Wolter,
he had overlooked nothing and provided
for everything. For example, he had more
than a hundred physical exhibits ready for
introduction at the proper time—fragments
of bone out of a fireplace where Wolter
tried to destroy his victim's body, a string of
fire-blackened, blue glass beads, a charred
scrap of embroidery from a shirtwaist, a
bent hatpin, a pathetically small gold finger
ring, part of a corset steel, a little wisp of
singed hair, even ashes and cinders of coal
and wood, each in a small wooden box, with
a sliding glass top. When Mr. Moss was
through with the identification of all these
things, he spread them out on a long table
in front of the jury box, where they stayed
for the best part of a week, as complete and
as satisfying and as grim a collection of
physical evidence as I ever saw produced
in a courtroom.

The sentiment of the community demanded a speedy trial for young Wolter, and he got it. It lasted from Monday morning until late Friday night, and all the way through it was packed as full of interest as the skin of a pawpaw is packed with pulp. At the press table we thought the big moment had been reached when Ruth Wheeler's sisters took the stand to tell of her departure from home on the last morning of her life, of their search for her that night after she failed to return, and, worst ordeal of all for them, to look at and touch some of the articles in the glass-topped little boxes. All of us marveled at the brave endurance that was shown by these two. Their hearts must have been near bursting, but neither of them wept nor broke down, and neither sought to tell what she believed rather than what she knew— the commonest failing of women witnesses. They did not show by look or word their feelings for Wolter. What they did show was an evident desire to tell the exact truth, without coloring or exaggeration.

I think no one who was there will ever

forget how Adelaide Wheeler looked. She was a slender, pretty girl, with a fair skin, which seemed dead white against the background of her black hat and black mourning gown, and a great coil of red hair on her head. One by one, she took the objects which Mr. Moss handed to her and in answer to his questions said, clearly and quietly: "Yes, I recognize this bow of ribbon. I tied it in Ruthie's hair myself that morning," or: "Yes, sir, I know this ring; it was my sister's and she gave it to Ruth on her sixteenth birthday. I would know it anywhere." Nearly everybody who was there wanted to cry, and great many did cry, when she took into her black-gloved hands an umbrella and said it had been her Christmas gift to Ruth. It was such a simple, plain, little black umbrella; just such a gift as good taste and a limited purse would have dictated.

But Wolter didn't cry. He stared at the dead girl's sister—only a year or two had separated the sisters in age and they were said to have looked very much alike—with a steady, insolent stare.

As I was saying just now, we reporters thought the big moment had come and gone when the sisters quit the stand, after perfunctory cross-examinations by Wolter's lawyers. But it hadn't. A little later that same day, Mr. Moss called as a witness for the State, Dr. George S. Huntington, the eminent anatomist, and now it developed for the first time that, with the consent of the mother, the body of Ruth Wheeler had been privately disinterred and given over to Dr. Huntington; and that he, after a series of wonderfully minute comparisons and measurements, was prepared to swear positively that the tiny pieces of bone found in the grate at the Seventy-fifth Street flat had belonged to the body which afterwards lay on the fire escape, so establishing the complete loop of evidence necessary to prove the corpus delicti, the body of the crime.

After the first flurry invariably excited by the appearance of an unexpected witness, the reporters slumped back in their chairs. As a rule, expert testimony doesn't make interesting reading, and we welcomed the prospect of a little respite from a strain that had been wearing us down fiercely all day. Presently it came out that Dr. Huntington, in dissecting the exhumed body, had found the missing left hand. All along we supposed that the left hand, like its fellow, had been cut off by the murderer and destroyed separately. Now we learned that the fire afterwards had burned the left arm in two, but that the hand was caught up under the shelter of the right arm hollow and escaped, practically intact. This point did not seem particularly important though, except as tending to show that the coroner's physicians had been hurried and possibly careless in performing the original autopsy. But Mr. Moss had something else in store.

William Travers Jerome, at once the most brilliant, the most daring and the most spectacular prosecutor I ever saw anywhere, would have worked up the denouement which was now at hand with studied care. He would have paved the way for his climax as skilfully as a trained playwright. James W. Osborne would have done the same thing; for Osborne, like Jerome, has the dramatic instinct highly developed. Moss, however, was of a different stamp, as methodical as a knitting machine and about as showy, but certain sure.

Slowly, as if unaware of the sensation he was about to unloose, Mr. Moss produced the skeleton of the little hand which Dr. Huntington had found. It was articulated and mounted in one of the glass-topped cases. The box was handed up to the witness casually and identified by him. The expert sat at ease, holding the box in his lap.

"Doctor," said Moss, droningly, "did you, in the course of the examinations which you have described, find anything in Exhibit K for identification—this hand?"

"I did."

"What did you find, please?"

"I found clutched in this hand six human hairs."

"What was the general condition of those six human hairs?"

"They were partly burned—that is, the ends of them had been scorched away."

"Did those hairs, in your opinion, come

from the head of the body which you dis-
sected?"

"They did not. They were of a different
texture and a different color."

"That is all, Doctor," said Mr. Moss, and
sat down.

For the smallest part of a minute there
was a hush, and then a stir ran through the
room like a breeze blowing suddenly into
tree tops. The reporters put their heads
down and began to write like mad, turning
out rush copy, forty or fifty sprawled words
to the sheet. For they knew, and the jurors
knew, and all there knew, that if there were
hairs clutched in Ruth Wheeler's fingers
and they were not from her own head, they
must have been torn from the head of the
man who killed her. She could not have
been killed by a chance blow—a suggestion
upon which Wolter's counsel had been
pinning his hopes of a mistrial or a com-
promise verdict. She must have met her
death in a struggle, fighting for her life.
Literally, Ruth Wheeler's dead hand had
risen out of the grave to convict her murderer.

As I ground out my story I snatched a quick look at Wolter. He made me think of a white worm, singed by a flame. He was physically shriveling up. "Rita," the English novelist, who had attended every session of the trial, was sitting just behind me. "Oh, the litle beast—the vile little beast!" I could hear her whispering to herself, over my shoulder.

From that moment there was never any doubting what Wolter's finish would be with that jury. Under cross-examination the next day he tripped and tangled himself in fifty places, and once he teetered on the edge of a confession; but nothing that he might have said or done could have added to, or abated from the effect of that bit of testimony by Dr. Huntington. Late of a Friday night the jurors came in and, while Wolter's old mother listened in a dumb agony, uncomprehendingly, for she knew no English, the prisoner looked upon his jurors and the jurors looked upon the prisoner, and the foreman said, "Guilty." A day or two later I met one of the jurymen, and he said to me:

"It was the evidence of that little girl's dead hand that convicted Wolter. After that, I don't think there was any doubt in the mind of a single one of us."

I recall one murder trial from which no one big thing stands out in relief as the memory of it rolls in my mind, because all the way through it was made up of climaxes and thrills, lapping one on the other. This was the first trial of Harry K. Thaw for the murder of Stanford White. Editors and reporters are forever dreaming of the perfect murder story, which will be the story of a young and pretty woman, preferably an actress, accused of killing a rich man by poisoning him, with a lot of mystifying features and complications to go along with it. When this comes to pass, if it ever does, it will be, from the standpoint of public interest (which means circulation, a matter of all importance to newspapers) a faultless story. Lacking such, the next best thing from a newspaper reporter's viewpoint was the case of this young millionaire spendthrift, already known everywhere for his freaks of extravagance, killing a famous genius, on account of a rarely beautiful woman, upon the top of New York's most noted building, a building which was itself a creation of the victim, during the opening performance of a summer roof garden show, with an audience of Broadway first-nighters for eyewitnesses. If there were missing from the crime any of the elements which go to make up a great newspaper story, the trial which followed provided an ample plenty. On the day Evelyn Nesbit Thaw, show girl and artist's model and town beauty, took the witness stand and told her wonderful narrative with such a wonderful dramatic effect and finish, the correspondent of one of the big London papers sent his paper more than five thousand words—sent it by cable at regular trans-Atlantic toll rates from a temporary cable office that had been fitted up in the corridor of the court-house. Nobody ever took the pains to figure out how many hundreds of columns of the proceedings the New York papers printed, nor how many square miles of pictures they carried. I know that there were between seventy-five and eighty reporters, special writers and artists in constant attendance. As a reporter for one of the New York afternoon papers I wrote in long hand a total of more than 500,000 words of running report—enough words to make eight sizable summer novels. And I was only one of the evening newspaper reporters there.

From a reporter's point of view you couldn't beat that trial as a continuing story. There was something to write about every minute. There was the money that was poured out, by the Thaw family, and sucked up, like water in a sand bed. People always like to read about vast sums being spent on a defense. There was the battle of the insanity experts—and the list of them was a directory of the high-priced alienists of the East—which lasted, off and on, a month. There was the line of divisions in the family pew, as we called the long row of seats set aside for the kin of the prisoner; at one end the white-haired, proud old mother and her daughter Alice, Countess of Yarmouth, the printing of whose title gave a daily garnish to the story; and at the other end Evelyn Nesbit Thaw in her navy blue school girl costume, "her testimony clothes;" always with her little actress friend at her side—a "wounded bluebird and a Broadway sparrow," one of the descriptive writers dubbed them. There were the Exaggerated Ego, the Dementia Americana, Dr. Brinton D. Evans' Brain Storm, and all the rest of the alienists' picturesque jargon. There was the savor of the stage and the studio; the weird revels of certain so-called rich Bohemians; the by-trails which led to the inner offices of certain jackals of the law—the upcroppings of the East Side gangs and the Fifth Avenue palaces; the family skeletons which marched out of hidden family closets in a grinning procession; the thread of intrigue which ran all through the theme, stringing the plots and the scandals together like beads on a wire. All these things, and each of them, helped to make a murder trial that ran at high tension, without sagging or lull.

Finally, there was the intellectual fight between the two leading lawyers, and this in itself furnished one of the big features,

if not the biggest, of the whole trial. For
the State—Jerome, quick and catlike in his
bodily movements; a veritable needle-gun
in his mental play; reaching his conclusions
with the mechanical precision and swiftness
of a cash register or a patent adding machine; terse, abrupt, snappish, yet when the
spirit moved and the occasion suited, in-
dulging in outgushing floods of denuncia-
tory eloquence fit to make your scalp crawl
under your hair. For the Defense—Del-
mas, almost the last notable survivor of the
old Southern and Western school of silver
tongues; imported, like a grand opera star,
at tremendous cost from his own Pacific
Slope to dazzle a jury of matter-of-fact
New York business men; suave, courteous,
stately; a coiner of sonorous phrases; wearing his frock coat and his forelock long;
rings on his fingers and bells on his voice;
and a tongue forked for biting sarcasm.

But, after these years it is not the war
between those two great lawyers, nor the
fuddled prisoner at the bar, nor the Woman
in the Case that stands out clearest in my
memory; it is two trivial incidents, one

pathetic, the other funny, that I remember best. One of these recollections centers about a physician who was called by the defense as their first witness. One of Thaw's massive battery of lawyers—it has since been conceded that he had several times as many as he needed—made the mistake of undertaking to qualify this gentleman as an expert in insanity and then, having committed that blunder, piled a worse one on top of it by putting to him a hypothetical question framed on the evidence of the other side. Undoubtedly the witness was a practitioner of standing and ability in his home community. But he was no alienist. And when it came time to cross-examine, it didn't take Jerome a minute to find this out. Always a relentless cross-examiner, he went at the witness blood raw. He ripped him to pieces and danced on the scraps. Before our eyes the witness sat there and visibly lost flesh. At first it was funny; then it was lamentable; then it was pitiful. For weeks thereafter an unhappy family physician was hanging about the court room seeking what he called a vindication and begging the lawyers for Thaw to put him back on the stand and give him a chance to explain. Finally, with the consent, I think, of Jerome himself, a point was somehow waived and it was entered on the record and printed in the papers that Dr. So-And-So had never really intended to pose as an expert. That night the doctor packed his grip and went home happy. I've never seen him since, but I haven't forgotten that woe-begone face and that drooping figure.

The other incident was one which occurred while the jury was being selected. Selecting a jury for a big murder trial is one of the things which seem to the layman a tiresome waste of time and words. Of a morning when the lawyers are feeling fresh and aggressive, they are overly particular in sifting the panel for material for the jury box. They tire themselves out asking questions and tire the talesmen out, too. They sound each man upon his personal views on every subject even remotely connected with the issue. They are overly cautious about accepting men as jurors and just as

cautious about rejecting them. But as the
day wears on and they wear out, the lawyers
grow less and less particular. Men are
promptly accepted who, earlier in the day,
would have been as promptly passed.
Watch the progress of the next big murder
trial that takes place in this country and see
if I am not right—see if the majority of the
jurors are not sworn in late of afternoons
or just before the noonday recesses.

As I recall it now, we were on the second
week of jury-getting, and the box was still
not half filled. The novelty of this part of
it had worn off, and we men for the afternoon papers were sending in nothing except
short bulletins every half hour or so, just to
show that we had not gone to sleep on the
assignment. The reporter for one of the
German afternoon papers had the place at
the press table next to mine. On this morning he didn't show up. In his stead came
a middle-aged, severe-looking German
with a thick beard and a pair of those
double-lens convex glasses on his nose. He
looked as if he might be an exchange editor
or a sub-editor. He entered with a bustle,

took out a foreign-made fountain pen, squared himself to it, and began sending away page after page of copy by a relay of serious-minded German copy boys.

The lawyers were weeding out the talesmen fast. A solid-looking citizen mounted the stand and began to answer the customary opening questions touching on his qualifications—what he thought about capital punishment, how he regarded expert testimony as compared to other testimony, and the rest of it. The substitute from the German paper took a hurried glance over his shoulder at a solid citizen and turned to me.

"Who is dis person?" he inquired in a half whisper, poising his pen.

"Just a talesman," I answered indifferently.

"Dalesmann?" he repeated. "Dalesmann? That's a Cherman name. Vot is dis Mr. Dalesmann's initials?"

"I don't know his initials," I said, "and 'talesman' is not his name. Talesman is what he is. He's merely being examined for service on the jury, you know."

"Ach, so," he said, blandly, "und I thought he vas a vitness," and went calmly on writing.

I've often wondered if his paper printed the copy that he had been sending in all the morning.

At the time when Mrs. Howard Gould, Katherine Gould, the actress that was, and her husband were fighting each other in the courts, we sat and listened to talk about vast sums of money until we grew sick and tired of writing dollar marks and numerals into our copy. Finally there came to the witness stand one blistering, hot afternoon a tall, solemn coachman, a Swede, who had once been employed at Castle Gould, the great Long Island estate of the two litigants. His testimony concerned certain alleged outbreaks of violent temper by Mrs. Gould. He narrated with painful care an occasion when she had accused one of the grooms of being drunk and had ordered his discharge on the spot.

"Well," asked Lawyer DeLancey Nicoll, "was he intoxicated?"

"Hay?"

"I say, was this groom you speak of intoxicated? Was he drunk?"

"No," said Ohmans slowly, "his name it bane O'Shaunnessy. But he not bane drunk."

Mr. Justice Victor Dowling, the trial judge, a most dignified man and himself of Irish descent, bent his head and shook with suppressed laughter. Everybody else laughed, too; everybody except Ohmans.

The first trial of ex-State Secretary Caleb Powers for the murder of William Goebel, governor of Kentucky, more than twenty years ago, was in a good many ways the most unique murder trial that has ever taken place in this country. Powers was the first, of all the men charged with the conspiracy to assassinate Goebel, to be put on trial. The State of Kentucky, always mighty fervent, politically, hung then on the raw edge of civil war. The people of the state were divided into two hostile camps. One faction regarded Powers as the head and front of the successful plot to kill from ambush the Democratic leader of the state. and clamored for his conviction. The other faction called him a martyr to political and personal prejudices; declared that he was being sacrificed to the demand for a victim merely because he chanced to be prominent among the younger Republicans, and demanded his acquittal as an innocent and an injured man.

On a change of venue, the trial took place at Georgetown, one of the prettiest of the smaller cities of the Blue Grass country, in an old-fashioned, hermetically-sealed, air-tight court-house, in the middle of a scorching hot summer. There were twenty-three lawyers in the case, eleven for the prosecution and twelve for the defense. They were the pick of the criminal bar of the state, and every one of them was a stalwart Goebel Democrat, an active anti-Goebel Democrat, or a partisan Republican. Each lawyer had a bitter personal enemy on the other side; some of them were quite generous in their hates and had two or three apiece. The trial judge, stern, handsome old Judge Cantrill, one of the last of the company commanders of Morgan's Raiders, and an un-reconstructed Confederate, had his private quarrels with at least two of the lawyers for the defense, and they were good haters, both of them, who repaid the debt with compound interest, and carried hair-trigger tempers besides. Many of the witnesses from the eastern end of the state were talented gun fighters, who had been reared in what has been called the Pure Feud Belt. As between them and the police force of the town the old antagonism between mountaineers and lowlanders was emphasized. The Blue Grass farmers who swarmed into the town and packed the court-house were ready to take a hand in the fighting if anybody else kindly would start it. A hip pocket that didn't bulge with hardware made in New England was a scarce thing. Finally Judge Cantrill stationed deputies at the doors to search every man who entered for concealed weapons. To show his own fair mindedness in the matter, the Judge himself submitted to being searched twice daily.

The finish of the trial came in the hottest, driest part of August. The summing-up required a full week with night sessions. There were ten speeches in all, five to a side, and not a single speaker took less than six hours. Kentuckians love courthouse oratory, and they came from all over the state for this feast of it. The sweltering little courtroom was jammed. Men and boys roosted in the narrow window openings, shutting out any breath of air that might have found its way in there. The reporters perched about anywhere—back of the jury box, on the steps of the judge's platform and up against the wall, writing their stories on lapboards and box tops. With true Southern courtesy, the sheriff had invited them to give up their seats to the ladies of the town, adding that they might just as well be nice and obliging about it, seeing that they were going to give them up anyhow. So we gave them up and fought with the populace each morning for such places as we could take by main force; then worked eight or ten or twelve smoking hours with our coats off and our collars unbuttoned and our shirts unfastened at the throats.

At the wind-up we sat under rival human

geysers which spouted forth vast streams
of those two favorite brands of Southern
eloquence—the fiery and the flowery—
night and day for one solid week. In the
acute stress of their personal emotions, some
of the orators forgot about the case and devoted their time to blasting their enemies
over the way. I remember how old Governor Brown looked, swelling himself up
with rage and contempt until he seemed
nine feet tall, and spilling molten lava, hot
ashes and the powdered pumicestone of his
wrath all over his chief adversary, Colonel
Thomas C. Campbell. The Governor always was a volcanic sort of speaker, anyhow.

Colonel Campbell, though, was a veteran
of a hundred court-house battles himself;
he only sat and smiled pleasantly through
Governor Brown's speech. And when his
turn came, he did a little blistering and
blasting himself. He was particularly bitter against the Louisville & Nashville Railroad, which had fought the dead Goebel,
and against General Basil M. Duke, of
Louisville, who had handled the railroad's

political and legislative affairs. Colonel Campbell charged that the L. & N. was indirectly responsible for the assassination of Goebel.

"I would give my right arm," he declaimed theatrically, "to get Basil Duke here on this witness stand."

"And give your other arm and both your legs to let him go again, suh," audibly growled an excited old gentleman in a front seat, breathing hard through his nose and glaring. The old gentleman had fought under Duke in Morgan's cavalry and he was prepared to fight again. The Judge, who, you will remember, was one of Morgan's raiders himself, rapped for order, but he didn't fine anybody for contempt of court. I don't believe such a trial could have taken place in any state of the Union except in Kentucky, and not in Kentucky except under the most extraordinary circumstances.

I don't know how much of the evidence the jury of dazed farmers and tobacco planters still carried in their minds as they filed out one day at noon; but it took them only forty minutes to frame a verdict of guilty, and Powers listened to it calmly, while sniffing at a tuberose which a young woman handed to him just as the foreman stood up.

But before we reached the verdict there occurred the scene which I started out to describe. In order to complete its case against Powers, the prosecution deemed it highly necessary to show that the bullet which killed Goebel was fired from a certain window of Powers's own office, in the department of the Secretary of State, on the grounds of the State Capitol at Frankfort. There were plenty of witnesses ready to testify that the sound of the shot seemed to come from that particular point; but sound is deceptive, and the lawyers for the Commonwealth were anxious to strengthen this defect in their chain of proof by better evidence. One morning there walked into their consultation room at one of the two Georgetown hotels a stranger, who told them something which so filled them with joy that fifteen minutes later when court opened they put him on the stand, without waiting to verify his story. This stranger was a short and stoutish man, with a long, flowing, sandy mustache, a round, pink nose and a pair of rolling blue eyes. His hair was thin in front but long and wavy behind. His whole front was spangled over with lodge emblems. On his coat lapel there was pinned a gold axe, which didn't lack so very much of being life size. Then and thereafter, during all his appearances, he clung fast to a tightly rolled umbrella. He looked like a cross between a corn doctor and a traveling book canvasser, and there was about him something that was funny and yet pathetic.

As he stood to be sworn, clutching his precious umbrella in his free hand, Charley Michaelson, who had been sent down there from New York to cover the story for the Hearst papers, leaned over and said to me: "In every big murder trial at least one volunteer perjurer turns up. This fellow here is a candidate for the job."

It was the first big trial I had ever covered, and I bent and asked him what made him think so.

"I can't tell you," said Michaelson, "but after a while you get to know them. I'll make a little bet I'm right."

The new witness was named Weaver. He had been a barber, he said, but had abandoned barbering to become an organizer of fraternal lodges with a roving commission; hence his heavy display of emblems. He had come to Frankfort on the day of the shooting; he had been strolling about the Capitol grounds looking at the buildings when he heard several shots fired rapidly and saw a man fall; he had looked then in the direction whence the sound of the firing came and had seen the barrel of a rifle protruding from the lower left-hand window of Caleb Powers' suite of offices. No, there couldn't be any mistake about it; he had seen the rifle barrel plainly, two feet or more of it; had seen the smoke coming out of its muzzle; had watched it as it was withdrawn and had seen hands of unseen bodies fumbling with the sash and closing the window. That was all; the other side might cross-examine.

On the cross-examination Weaver suf-

fered somewhat. What business had
brought him to Frankfort? No business
at all—he just happened by and stopped off
to see the Legislature in session. Did he
tell anybody what he had seen before he
left Frankfort? No, he couldn't say that
he had. Why not? He couldn't say that
either. How long a time did he spend on
the Capitol grounds before the shooting occurred? Oh, a good while, two hours,
maybe two hours and a half. What had he
been doing all that time? Strolling around.
Just strolling? Yes, that was it—just
strolling. Wasn't it snowing hard that
morning? Well, it had snowed some.
Didn't he mind the snow? Oh, no, he had
his umbrella with him. The same umbrella which he now held in his hand? The
same. And so on for more than an hour.
Judge James Sims, as cross-examiner, managed to worry the stroller a good deal, but
he couldn't show anywhere that Weaver
had any prejudice against Powers or any
motive for testifying to anything except the
truth.

The impression among the jurors must

have been that this was a well-meaning,
rather simple-minded person who might
get tangled up on the incidental details of
his testimony, but who would not, know-
ingly, state a falsehood under oath.
Eventually, Judge Sims had to let him go.
Weaver remained around town, basking in
the temporary limelight, like a kitten before a grate fire.

That night the circulation manager of
one of the Louisville papers slipped into
Georgetown, bringing with him a troupe
of leather-lunged city newsboys and a special edition of his paper. The front page
of this special edition was entirely devoted
to the display, under appropriately large
heads and subheads, of these indisputable
facts:

On the day of the shooting and almost on
the hour, the witness, Weaver, had been in
a town away off at the other end of the state
from Frankfort, organizing a lodge and in-
vesting its officers with their high-sounding
titles and teaching them the ritual. When
word of the shooting reached this town, he
had made quite a speech on the enormity

of such a thing, and then he had gone with
certain of his newly-made brothers to the
telegraph office in the hope of learning
fuller particulars of the assassination.
Finally, a special train was then on its way
to Georgetown, bearing practically the entire membership of the lodge. In the
morning, bright and early, they were there
—the Supreme King, the Puissant Imperial
Potentate, the Keeper of the Royal Rolls,
and all the rest, bringing with them books
and archives, showing time, place and date.

I think most of us began our stories that
morning something after this fashion:

"The Strolling Barber took another
stroll to-day, strolling from the county
courthouse to the county jail, and thence
into a cell. He was accompanied by his
umbrella and the sheriff of the county."

Just as Michaelson told me then, there is
at least one of them who turns up at every
big trial. It is rare that they really have a
criminal motive in testifying to something
which never happened, or which they never
saw; some of them, I am convinced, really
get to believe they are telling the truth.

They are the same people who write the crank letters; love of notoriety amounts to an obsession with them.

The trial of Henry Youtsey, a state house clerk, for complicity in the Goebel murder, followed closely on the trial of Powers and, like the Powers trial, it was held at Georgetown. When it was perhaps a third done, the judge fixed a day on which, following the local procedure, the prisoner, the jurors and one lawyer from either side would go to Frankfort in a body to view the scene of the crime and the surroundings. One of the reporters covering the story at Georgetown had just married. He knew the regular Frankfort correspondent of his paper would cover the Frankfort end of the trip, and he desired greatly to steal a holiday and take his bride up to Cincinnati for a day. He went to see Judge Cantrill, and Judge Cantrill told him that after the return from Frankfort, court would probably adjourn for the day, since it would be late in the afternoon anyhow when the party got back. So the reporter and his bride felt perfectly safe in slipping away.

The day at Cincinnati stretched into a day and a night. A famous actress was playing a dramatized version of the most popular novel of the hour at one of the theaters, and, since nothing would be happening anyhow at Georgetown, Mr. and Mrs. Reporter decided to stay over, see the play and catch an early train which would land them in Georgetown in time for the opening of court. When they reached the station the next morning, the husband bought a morning paper. It was the Cincinnati *Enquirer*. In those days the *Enquirer* ran to large, deep, single-column headlines. The reporter took one look at the last column of the first page of his *Enquirer,* and his knees knocked together.

Under a Georgetown date line he read that, unexpectedly, a night session of the trial had been arranged. About ten o'clock, Arthur Goebel, the younger brother of the murdered Governor, had taken the stand as a witness and had proceeded to tell for the first time in any court the story of a detailed confession of the crime and the conspiracy, as made to him by Youtsey four months

before in the Frankfort jail on the day of
Youtsey's arrest—a confession of which no
one on earth, with the exception of a few
persons in Arthur Goebel's confidence, had
any knowledge. To the newspaper men it
had come as an absolute surprise. But this
wasn't all. As Arthur Goebel, acting out
the scene in the jail, with minute detail,
reached the point where he began word for
word to repeat Youtsey's confession, Youtsey leaped to his feet, screaming out that
Goebel was not dead and all the devils in
Hell couldn't kill him, and then, as the
court officers jumped forward to overpower
him, fell on the floor writhing about and
frothing at the mouth, finally going off into
a strange stupor and lying like one dead.
Youtsey's young wife had gone into hys-
terics at the sight of her apparently fren-
zied husband fighting with the officers and
being held down and handcuffed. Several
women had fainted. In a stampede to get
out of the narrow room, persons had been
crushed at the doors and on the narrow
stairs. And then, while Youtsey, mute and
seemingly unconscious, lay on a cot along-

side the witness stand, with his eyes set in his head and his chained hands crossed on his breast, Arthur Goebel, who had not moved once during all the uproar, had gone calmly on with his amazing, totally unexpected testimony.

All that had happened at Georgetown the night before—with a new reporter on his first big assignment ninety miles away in Cincinnati. Because the hour had been so late and the wires so crowded, the story in the morning paper was little more than a series of jerky bulletins; but his paper was an afternoon paper at Louisville, and he knew the office would be expecting a complete account of the whole thing, testimony and all, for the first edition, going to press at 11.10.

The train was one of those things misnamed an accommodation train, which meant that it stopped at all stations and hesitated in between. The reporter walked the aisle of his car in a condition which fluctuated between a fever and a chill. It seemed to him that only slow, fat, old ladies

got off and only slow, decrepit, old gentlemen got on.

The train deliberated across the Blue
Grass uplands. It crawled and crept. It
was due at Georgetown at 10.30. Following the usual custom, it was late. It was
ten minutes before eleven when the loco-
motive whistled for Georgetown. As the
train dawdled into the station, a newly married newspaper reporter, basely deserting
his bride of a month, leaped off the rear
platform, ripped up the cindered right-of-
way with his toes and knees, gathered himself up and tore down Main Street toward
the Western Union office as fast as a moderately long pair of legs would carry him.
As he fell panting in at the open door of
the telegraph office, the manager looked up,
startled.

"Where in thunder you been?" he asked.
"Looky here—I got about a thousand
messages for you from the office already
this morning," and he held up a double
handful of the little yellow envelopes.

"What did you do?" gasped a despairing

voice which the exhausted reporter recognized as slightly resembling his own.

"Well," said the manager with appalling deliberation, "I couldn't find you and I couldn't find any of the other boys that had time to help out—all of them was busy with their own stuff. And your folks was calling for copy every half minute and not getting any."

"Oh, Lord!"

"So, not knowing what else to do and feeling that something had oughter to be done, I took a chance. I went up to the hotel and got a copy of Clarence Walker's transcript of what happened last night, and about three-quarters of an hour ago I put it on the wire. It was sort of long—over four thousand words, I guess; but I couldn't think of anything else."

"Let me see it, quick," said the reporter.

"Too late now," drawled the manager. "Bancroft's just sending the last page in over your office wire.

The reporter ran around behind the screen and scooped up the pile of typewritten sheets which lay just under the operator's busy right elbow. He ran his eyes through one page, through another, part way through a third—and his heart, which had been a cast-iron hitching post down in the pit of his stomach, jumped back up in his chest where it belonged and turned into a living vital organ again. For it was a great story that had gone into the home office. Done in the official style of the methodical, unemotional court stenographer it was all there—the oaths, the screams, the inarticulate cries, the orders of the judge, the ravings of Youtsey, the testimony of young Arthur Goebel, everything—and told so it made a more graphic picture of the scene than any written-out, descriptive account could possibly have been.

The reporter went back and found his wife and resumed normal breathing. Later in the day, he got a telegram of congratulation from his editor. With a fifty-word introduction, written in the office, the stenographic narrative had run in the paper exactly as it came in over the wire. And it had been the talk of the town. So far as anybody in Louisville knew, no paper had ever before covered such a story in such a way. The admiring managing editor wondered how the reporter ever came to think of it.

The reporter didn't tell him. I happen to know, because I was the reporter.

CHAPTER SEVEN

———

Leaves Out of My Thrill Book

CHAPTER VII

Leaves Out of My Thrill-Book

INTO every working reporter's life come big thrills—outstanding moments which burn forever after, like red-hot asterisks, in his memory. Usually he experiences them in the line of his journalistic duties. His job takes him to places where exciting things occur and he gets tangled up in them. Preparing copy for this book I've been trying, as I went along, to conjure up memories of my own biggest thrills—not the thrills of private life; that would be a different matter, but what you might call professional thrills.

Once upon a time I went up in a German war balloon with a German military observer for a traveling companion and from an altitude of 1200 feet looked down upon the first Battle of the Aisne. I was told at the time that I was the only civilian who had been permitted to take a trip in one of the German war-balloons. We didn't stay aloft very long. A French aeroplane showed itself in our quarter of the horizon and to the accompaniment of booming anti-aircraft guns we were hauled back to earth again. But we did stay aloft long enough for me to have a series of such tingles as rarely come to an ordinary writing person. The thing had its humorous aspect, its serio-comic aspect and one which was downright tragic.

Elsewhere in this volume I have described how three of us in the latter part of 1914 got a pass from the Kaiser to go to the front. That was the beginning of a crowded month for us. In the course of our wanderings under escort we reached the Aisne. The great battle which was to wage for so many months between the Allies and the Central European powers was starting along that historic stream. On a gorgeous September morning we rode in a staff car from corps headquarters in the ancient city of Laon to where the Kaiser's

armies were digging themselves in along
the plateaus and the valleys seven miles to
the southward. Eventually we came upon
this German observation balloon, which
was anchored in a hillside meadow over-
looking the British positions. After a considerable amount of telephoning, permis-
sion was given that one of us might make
an ascent in the balloon in order to view
the battle lines and the artillery operations
then going on. The choice fell upon me.
I nominated myself, seconded the nomination, moved that the nominations be closed
and then voted for myself. It's a good way
to carry an election. I recommend it.

My companion on the trip was a bearded
young captain from Cologne who spoke
fairly good English but whose mental processes, as I shortly thereafter discovered,
were fashioned strictly on Teutonic lines.
The basket in which we were to soar aloft
was but not much larger than the average
clothes hamper is and it was rather with
difficulty that the two of us wedged ourselves into it, standing back to back.

Now, going up in a balloon to spy on his

enemy and to run a chance of being brought down in flames by hostile aircraft was all a part of the day's work to my basket-mate. But to me the experience promised sensation and novelty. I had never before ridden in a balloon, captive or otherwise. I had never before seen such extensive military operations. And to the best of my knowledge and belief I never before had had such frosted feet.

As the soldier crew paid out our tether and we climbed upward into the air, swinging gently under the great sausage-shaped bag of hot air above us, the captain addressed me over his shoulder and in the tone of one striving to make conversation with a stranger, said:

"It is too bad that I did not loan you one of my uniform overcoats before we left the earth."

"Oh, that's all right, Captain," I answered striving to appear cheery and comfortable. "This overcoat I have on is plenty warm, I imagine."

"Quite so," he said, "but it is not of a military cut and it has no shoulder straps."

"What difference does that make?" I asked in my innocence.

"Well, you see," he explained politely, "the situation is like this: If the wire rope which holds us should break—which I trust it may not—and if we should descend in the enemy's lines as undoubtedly we would unless the wind changed—which is not probable—to me they would give the honors of war as a captured officer but you, undoubtedly, they would shoot immediately on the spot as a civilian spy who had no business to be there."

I pondered this for a space. Then he spoke again, in reassuring tones.

"But, my friend," he said, "I should give myself no concern on that account if I were you."

"No?" I said. "That's nice."

"Yes," he said, "you need not feel distress; because if the cable should break the chances are as a hundred to one that we should both be quite dead long before we came down."

So then I saw there was no occasion for worry on my part and we continued to climb into the heavens. When we had reached an altitude of perhaps a thousand feet the cable checked us and our smooth upward course suddenly changed to a bumpy, jerky, swaying motion very like that of a small boat tossed in rough waters.

Again he spoke, comfortingly. "I trust," he said, "you are not being discommoded. Very often when that happens which is now happening, even an experienced balloon-observer becomes ill. You are not seasick, eh?"

"No," I said truthfully, "but I don't mind telling you in confidence that I'm just a trifle homesick."

About that time a French aeroplane appeared in the heavens and circled toward us and the crew yanked us hurriedly to the earth. That night at dinner I overheard the young captain speaking to his commander, General Von Herringen, of my balloon trip with him. He spoke in German but I knew enough of the language—a fact of which he was not aware—to gather his meaning.

"The Americans are a curious people," he said with all seriousness. "I had thought, inasmuch as Herr Cobb had never seen a battle before, that he would be deeply interested in the sight presented to him when we had reached our extreme elevation. But at the moment when the whole panorama of the action is spread out beneath him I ask him what his sensations are and, strangely enough, he tells me that he is experiencing a great longing to behold once more his native land."

So much for the humorous phase of the experience. It had a side to it which was not in the least humorous.

After the lapse of these intervening years I still recall quite vividly a thing which happened after we had been drawn back to earth. With his camera, a fellow-correspondent had taken several snapshops of us—one of the German officer and me standing alongside the small wicker car of the balloon, two or three of the balloon starting up with the pair of us wedged together in the basket, and more snaps of the balloon coming hurriedly down. When we had descended, I turned to my late traveling companion and said:

"Herr Captain, I should be very glad to send you a set of these pictures if you would care to have them. My friend here will have the films developed as soon as we get back to Aix-la-Chapelle, and I know he will have no objection to my having some duplicate copies printed for you."

In his careful English the captain told me he would be very glad indeed to have such photographs and he thanked me and my confrère. Then he added:

"Now, on second thought, perhaps it would be better if you sent them to my mother at her home." And he gave me the name of a titled person, a baroness, as I recall, and an address in the city of Cologne.

"Very well," I said, "but I am sure they would reach you safely if I sent them by field post to staff headquarters at Laon."

"No," he said, "I think the better plan would be that you send them to my mother."

Still I did not get his point.

"I assume then," I said, "that you are thinking soon of going away from this place?"

He smiled quietly.

"In this service," he said, "we think always that soon we may be going away to quite altogether some other place."

He was right. A week later, coming that way again, I asked regarding him and was told that three days before a French flier had succeeded in dropping an inflammable bomb upon his balloon and that he had been burned to death in the air.

One glorious afternoon of early spring—this was in 1918, nearly four years later, when we had got into the war and I had gone back again to Europe as a correspondent—I asked a British sergeant if he knew where the Germans were. Really, I asked him more for talk's sake than for any other reason. I had no idea that they were close —I thought the nearest Germans must be at least two miles away. I had just joined him in a wrecked café in a little village on the banks of the Oise. Through a shell-hole in the northern wall of the building we could see the narrow river flowing, almost at our feet, and the bridge that spanned it, and three miles away the spires and towers of the old town of Noyon, which only

that day had fallen, after stubborn resistance, into the enemy's hands. The bridge
itself had been barricaded at a point about
midway of its length. On our side of the
barricade a half a company of French engineers were planting mines with a view to
blowing the structure up before the Germans in force could reach it.

This was the fourth day of the final great
German offensive. And this sergeant and
one mate, a private, were all that remained
of a company of a British infantry regiment.
So far as they knew, every other member
of their company, from the captain down,
had been killed, captured or wounded. For
four days and four nights they had been
under fire almost constantly. They had
been driven backward and backward like
chips upon a tidal wave, until finally these
two lone survivors had been flung out of the
main path of the advance and had landed
here in a side-eddy where for the moment
there was no heavy fighting. Yet it was the
point of contact for the French reserves,
hurrying up to join forces with the battered
remnants of the stubbornly-resisting, slowly-

retreating Britishers. This pair were gray with fatigue and staggering for lack of sleep and food. As it turned out, they were at least five miles away from the nearest organized body of British troops. But through all the hideous bedevilment they had clung to their arms and their equipments. The sergeant, as the ranking officer of his company, was in command over the private, who constituted in his turn the available strength of the company; and as the saying went in their army, they were still carrying-on.

"We've been a bit knocked abaht, sir," said the sergeant to me, "but we shall 'ave the best of 'em yet. As a matter of fact, sir, the beggars cahn't fight, you know."

I said to myself that even though the Germans might then be winning leagues of disputed French soil each day, and even though Gough's army had broken to bits before their onslaught as they made their great shove toward Paris, still, and in the long run, the Germans could never conquer the breed which produced a man of the type of this non-com.—a man who after what he had gone through yet could state, not in

boastfulness but only with the sincerity and
the confidence of a man expressing an in-
controvertible conviction, that the beggars
couldn't fight.

This remark from him, though, was to
follow after the incident I mean to narrate.
As I have said, I asked him, when I crept
into the ruined café which sheltered him
and his companion, if he knew where the
Germans were. I figured for myself that
they could not be so very many kilometres
away, but since I, with three others, had
just arrived upon the spot, coming in a tin
Lizzette from Soissons, and he seemingly
had been upon the ground some time, I assumed he might have direct information regarding the whereabouts of the enemy.

"Come with me, sir, if you please, sir,"
he said, simply.

I was bundled up in a uniform overcoat
and undoubtedly he mistook me for an
American officer. He picked up his rifle
and balanced it under his right arm and led
the way out of the side door of the house.
I followed him, wondering.

He escorted me to the foot of the little

street, past where French soldiers were crouched behind the shelters of broken walls and then we were out upon the bridge picking our way past the toiling, sweating engineers until we came to the barricade. It was no more than waist high, the barricade, so that the upper parts of our bodies made fair targets against a sunlit background. With his left hand he pointed toward the opposite bank of the river and in a most matter-of-fact tone he said:

"They're right there, sir, 'id in them 'azel bushes—abaht eighty yards away, sir, I should say. If you look close p'raps you can see them moving abaht."

As Heaven is my judge, I desired above all things to go immediately and with despatch away from there. To the very bottom of my soul I regretted my mad curiosity; but he had mistaken me for a soldier and for an American soldier at that. Except that I carried no badges of rank on my shoulder straps I wore the uniform of an American officer. Regardless of my private feelings I must live up to that uniform. Finally, that sense of self-respect, or that pose, or that whatever it is which makes a man less afraid of being killed than of having a stranger discover how desperately afraid he really is, kept me there. I trust that the cigar I held in my mouth did not tremble and that my voice was casual as I said:

"Well, if they're so close as all that why don't they take a potshot at us?"

Even as I spoke, I thought I could see through the thickish screen of bare branches at least two gray-clad figures slowly wriggling down nearer the water's edge, and, incidentally, nearer us.

"Well, you see, sir," he replied, "it's like this: the beggars probably think we cahn't see them from 'ere. There's only a few of them there yet and I tyke it they don't want to expose their position by shootin' this wye until they're a bit stronger. Was there anything else, sir?"

I told him there wasn't anything else and signified that we might as well be getting back to our late refuge and, at his side, I returned with him to where his private awaited us. The distance could not have been more than fifty yards yet at the time I mentally recorded it as being one of the longest walks in the annals of pedestrian exercises. For me the whole thing was replete with thrills. Indeed, fully forty-eight hours elapsed before the thrilled feeling abated within me.

Since we're on the subject of thrills, I am moved to record one which fell outside the professional lines and yet, in a way, was related to my calling in life. Until it came to pass it had never occurred to me that I might have the psychic gift. If I thought about the matter at all I thought of it as one having an appeal to persons who are slenderer than I am. Because it had seemed to me that those who went in for the occult usually were thin people. For example, I could fancy Madame Sarah Bernhardt being psychic but I could not conceive of former President Taft in that rôle. In other words it did not seem probable that one could successfully be psychic by the pound.

Be that as it may, I shall recite the incident and leave it to the reader to judge.

The time was September of 1913, and the place was Paris. It was the occasion of my first visit to that city. I had been sent there by the editor of *The Saturday Evening Post* to do some articles on the supposedly gay life; so, in a sense, it was a reportorial assignment. There were two of us traveling in company. Before we left London a friend had recommended to us that we lodge while in Paris at a hotel which was small but very good, as small hotels are apt to be in parts of Europe. So, before quitting London we wired ahead for reservations. At the time, we were not aware that this hotel was a favorite stopping-place for members of the nobility and even of royalty when desiring privacy and quiet on visits to the French capital. As it turned out, its guests then included the King of Greece, traveling incog, an Italian princess who featured her own private gold toothpick in the main dining-room at every meal, a Russian grand duke and a certain distinguished Englishwoman who bore a famous title and who was well known on both sides of the Atlantic Ocean as a person of the utmost social consequence. However, we did not learn that we were abiding in a very nest of nobility and notability until some hours after our arrival.

We reached Paris on a Saturday evening. That night we took in the life of the Boulevards, or as much of it as we could take in between eight o'clock and midnight. Next morning we saw the after-church parade of fashionable folk and rode through the Bois and in the afternoon went to the races at Longchamps. In the evening we were going to a theater and so, late in the afternoon, being pretty well fagged out, I went to my room to take a nap. Before lying down I drew the curtains to exclude the daylight but I made the mistake of not locking the outer door of my chamber. Presently I wakened out of a sound sleep to find that the electric lights had been flashed on and that a valet with a spade-shaped black beard was bending over the footboard of my bed and inquiring if there was anything he could do for Monsieur. I told him yes, there was; he could go and get a shave.

He turned out the lights and departed,

and I drifted off again to be aroused inside
of five minutes by another sudden illumina-
tion. This time the visitor was a venerable
char-woman carrying a broom and a bucket.
She had no English. I had no French. By
the use of sign language I persuaded her to
depart and then I got up and bolted the
door and went and lay down again. I was
determined to have my nap out. But sleep,
twice banished, would not return. I tried
the expedient of counting imaginary sheep
jumping over an imaginary fence. I kept
it up until the mere thought of sheep became absolutely abhorrent to me. I tried
repeating the alphabet backwards. With
each passing moment, though, I became
more completely and entirely awake.

Then the telephone, which stood on a
tabouret in a corner of the room, began to
emit curious sounds. It did not exactly
ring but it clicked and squeaked and gave
off muffled, jingling notes as though it
might be getting ready to ring. It was a
French telephone and therefore was intended more for ornamentation than for
utilitarian purposes. I had been warned in

advance against French telephones. Seasoned travelers had told me that when on the continent I wished to reach a person in a hurry the best method and the quickest would be to let the telephone strictly alone and send a messenger with a note.

So when my telephone began to stutter I turned upon it a dubious eye. "Surely," said I to myself, "surely that kindly destiny which rules our lives will not call upon me to try to speak over a French telephone with somebody who probably speaks nothing but French. I have lost my beauty-sleep, but I wish to keep what is left of my once sunny disposition." Just as I was saying that to myself the telephone quit rehearsing and rang intermittently, with abrupt breaks in the rhythm of its ringing as though the connection might be faulty or something.

I lay there hoping that the instrument would presently cure itself of what ailed it, but no, the ringing kept on. It became practically continuous. The clamor filled the room. So, finally I got up and I fitted the combination speaking-and-listening apparatus about my neck so that one opening was near my ear and the other opening was in front of my lips and I said, somewhat shortly:

"Well, what is it?"

Over the wire came a voice saying in English:

"Are you there?"

"No," I said, "I'm here."

"Quite so," said the voice. "You're there. Who is it wants Lady Upchurch?"

Taken though I was by surprise, I nevertheless rallied promptly.

"Well," I said, "I don't, for one."

The tone of the reply betokened a querulous insistence. Indeed, it was a demand rather than an invitation which came next:

"What! You don't want Lady Upchurch?"

"Well," I said, "if you're going to make an issue of it I might take the proposition under consideration. When did Her Ladyship start doing this sort of thing?"

The shock was such that my unseen interrogator forgot to ring off and evidently was too grievously stricken to make any direct response. But over the wire I could hear that voice murmuring to its dazed owner these words:

"Oh, God bless my soul! What a frightful bounder! What a frightful Yankee bounder! Oh, God bless my soul!"

Now, here comes the really significant and, from an occult standpoint, the interesting phase of the occurrence. At the very instant when the person at the other end of the wire spoke for the first time—before ever the lips of that person had framed the opening sentence, I, standing there alone in my room, had visualized him. The inflection in his voice and the depth of the tone told me it must be a man. The accent unmistakably had been that of an educated Englishman. But it was more than the vague figure of an Englishman that flashed before my vision. I saw him plainly revealed as a small and narrow-shouldered person in dark clothes, having the look about him, moreover, of being somebody's social secretary. As clearly as though he stood before me I saw that he had large and prominent front teeth and a pair of those outspreading, translucent ears, and I somehow knew that when he stood in the bright sunlight the rays of the sun would percolate through his ears as through the stained-glass windows of a memorial chapel and cast a soft diffused pinkish glow upon his face. I saw that customarily his mouth hung slightly ajar because of the presence of adenoids—not the small, domestic adenoids which we know in America, but the large fruity golden-russet adenoids of old England. I saw him as one shrinking and diffident and easily embarrassed. I saw him pigeon-toed. I saw that his trousers were a wee bit short for him in the legs and that the collar of his coat stood well away from his neck. In a flash I saw all this.

Now then, for the sequel: Two days later at the door of the hotel I, going out, narrowly escaped bumping into a person coming in. In every regard this person was the physical embodiment of the conjured image of that Sunday afternoon. There were the buck teeth, the membraneous mother-of-pearl ears, the retreating coat collar and all the rest of it, down to the minutest of preconceived details.

I addressed the proprietor of the hotel, who chanced to be standing near the door.

"That gentleman yonder," I said, "who is he?"

"I do not know ze gentleman's name," he said, "but he is ze private secretary of Lady Upchurch." The proprietor drew nearer to me and discreetly sank his voice to a conversational undertone: "I do not know why it is," he said, "but always ze private secretaries of rich English ladies look like zat one."

I have stated the circumstances exactly as I recall them. Having stated them I close this chapter by repeating the same question which I put some paragraphs back, namely:

Am I psychic or am I not?

Whether I am or am not, the suggestion coming, as it were, out of a clear sky that so distinguished a personage as Lady Upchurch was trying to date up with me—me, a simple, unostentatious, American newspaper man—gave me such a thrill as properly belongs, I hold, in an article devoted to personal thrills.

CHAPTER EIGHT

The Trail of the Lonesome Laugh

CHAPTER VIII

The Trail of the Lonesome Laugh

I AM in receipt of a favor of recent date from a distinguished magazine editor asking for the recipe for making people laugh, and in reply to same would beg to state as follows:

It can not be done.

To be sure, there are a few persons among the population who are ready to laugh, anyhow. You don't have to make them. It is a vice to which they are incurably addicted. They laugh for the same reason that a conch-shell makes a murmuring sound when you hold it up to your ear, being, like the shell, mostly hollow inside, and full of convolutions. They throw off laughter like a cave throwing off echoes. Their intentions are good, but their execution is bad.

This class includes the kind of person who, when you try to tell a funny story in company, starts laughing at the wrong place and spoils the point for you, because the others become so intent on looking down inside of him and wondering how a head that seems so shy on interior furnishings can possess such splendid acoustic qualities, that they forget to listen to you.

And, similarly, when he has read your little printed effusion, he goes around gurgling like the last pint of suds in a sink, buttonholing casual acquaintances and saying to them, "Say, old man, did you read the funny piece that this fellow What's-his-name wrote the other day? Let's see now— it went something like this, near as I can recall." And he strikes out and tries to tell it and gets all balled up and goes lame and remarks that, well, anyhow, it was funny as thunder the way that fellow put it, and staggers off, still overcome with maniacal mirth. Whereupon the casual acquaintance gives a low, deep grunt of disgust and departs, convinced in his own mind that the man who tried to tell him the story must be the biggest idiot in the known world, with the exception of the one who wrote it.

Even so, the man who stands prepared to laugh with you, with or without the proper provocation, is far, far outnumbered by the man who'd see you cold and laid out first. He defies you to make him laugh. He practically warns you in advance that if you get a laugh out of him it will be over his dead body. He doesn't know you, but he's your enemy for life.

Basing their calculations on the figures of the recent census, conservative judges have estimated that of this class there are upward of thirty-five millions in the United States, excluding Alaska and Porto Rico.

There remains still a third grand division; and to those kindly souls who compose it, in all loving respect and heartfelt gratitude I here take off my new hat—or will take it off when I get it—and say to them that they are the salt of the earth and the candy kids and the water on the wheel of every hard-working journeyman who holds a card in the Funny Men's Union and is blithesome to order, by the day, week, or job. These are the ones who pick up the paper or the magazine and finding your contribution, read it through, put it down, and say to themselves:

"Well, on the whole, that seems to me a pretty tolerably sad affair. But this same chap handed me one good laugh, I remember, back in the spring of the year that Coxey's Army came through, and another in the fall of nineteen-three, I think it was, and I guess he's doing the best he can. Maybe if I wrote him a little letter and told him to keep right on plugging along—because you never can tell when things are going to take a change for the better—it might brighten him up and make him more cheerful."

Sometimes they write the letter, too, and the sad-faced, despondent humorist takes it home, shows it to his wife, and pastes it in the scrap-book. I've known of good, durable wheezes that bore these dividends quarterly or oftener for years and years.

You may have noted that in making this classification, I have used the masculine gender exclusively. I have done so advisedly and after due thought, because all the best authorities on the subject agree that it is not in the nature of a woman to take a joke, for better or for worse, the first time she meets it face to face. In the matter of being shown, the average woman, so far as humor is concerned, is from so far out in Missouri that she's practically from Kansas. She is up on the tallest peak of the Ozark Mountains, very skeptical, not to say skittish. She wants to hear a thing that's funny several times and let it soak into her and mingle with her other ingredients; then after a suitable period of time she begins to care for it and forever after bears it a deep and lasting affection. At least, so the authorities affirm.

Once there was a woman who could see a joke the first time she came across it and who could carry the point in her mind and keep it in its proper relation and proportions to the rest of the joke. But she is no more. She lived a great while ago, back in the Middle Ages, I think it was, and she was put to death as a witch. The police authorities of that period didn't exactly know what it was that was wrong with her and peculiar about her, but they could tell there was something very, very uncanny and unusual in her mental make-up somewhere, so they followed the customary procedure in vogue at the time and burned her at the stake. At least, so I have been told. I think Finley Peter Dunne is the funniest man in the world, but I know a woman, a very bright woman she is, too, who reads his stuff only because she has seen his picture and thinks he has a nice face. She prefers the funny things that were printed in a red-bound book called "Gems of American Wit and Humor," which she has been acquainted with from childhood and knows by heart.

Of course, there are things which are naturally and inevitably funny, and which carry their appeal to all the grades of society. But these, alas! mainly belong to the humor of the stage and not to the humor of the printed page. Still I never yet met a comedian who didn't think he would be infinitely funnier than he was if he could only take his pen in hand and write his fun instead of acting it. If he only knew!

When a comedian hasn't any funny written lines to speak, he can fall back on the funny physical lines which a kindly nature gave him, and still keep his audience roaring. I have seen this done myself, often. Give your comedian an educated ear that he can fan himself with, or a gifted pair of legs that bow outward and look like a Gates Ajar design when he walks up-stage, or a pair of talented eyebrows and an automatic Adam's apple, and it is enough. The ushers will be coming down and warning stout persons to laugh with less abandon or else kindly stop by the box-office on their way out and get their money back.

But the writing person does not look funny while in the act of dashing off those quaint conceits which are copied in all the papers and credited to somebody else. Believe me, on the contrary.

I know a man who is one of the funniest writers in the business—at least, his admirers say he is funny. Of course, none of his fellow funny writers would say so. That would be highly unprofessional and contrary to all the ethics. But among a considerable number of outsiders he has the reputation of being genuinely funny. And when he sits down at his typewriter and slips a clean, unsullied sheet of paper into the machine, his associates glance inquiringly at him; and if a look of intense pain comes stealing over his face; and if his brows knit together in deep corrugations, and his gills begin to pant up and down with slow, convulsive movements, and he emits low, groaning sounds, then those who cannot bear the sight of suffering arise and tiptoe off, saying to one another as they go:

"Come, let us go away from here. Our poor friend is getting ready to write something funny."

Now with the stage humorist, as I have already said, the conditions are vastly different. A comedian can do the same things and say the same things over and over again, night after night. If a writer uses his own best quip oftener than twice per annum, some unpleasant busybody with a scrapbook or a good memory will draw the deadly parallel on him and shoot him down on the wing. For better purposes of comparison I have gone to the trouble of compiling a list of some of the funniest things on the stage. The list is as follows:

1.   When a performer starts to move and the trap drummer in the orchestra scrapes a resined piece of cord so that the comedian thinks his clothes are splitting.

2.   When an Irish monologist speaks a sentence in Yiddish.

3.   When a clown acrobat poises himself to jump a tremendous distance and then suddenly changes his mind and walks off.

4.   When a comedian starts to sing and the trombone player sounds a discord, causing the comedian to stop and look at him threateningly.

5.   When a low comedian, in leaving the stage, walks up against something solid and hits his nose.

6.   When a monologist, contemplating the street scene on the back drop behind him, says, "Ah, Philadelphia on a busy day!"

7.   When he looks in the window of a house painted on the scenery and pretends to see something funny going on.

8.   When the black-face half of a musi-

cal team takes off eight or nine waistcoats of different colors in rapid succession.

9. When a dancing comedian trips on something, and then stoops down and picks up an ordinary pin.

10. When a character comedian turns around and shows a red bandanna handkerchief pinned in the tails of his frock coat.

11. When a comedy character wears white spats fastened with large pearl buttons, and a high hat.

12. When a comic countryman runs his fingers through his chin whiskers and makes a whistling sound between his teeth, suggestive of the night wind soughing through a weeping-willow tree.

Personally, I think white spats are almost the funniest things one sees on the stage. Whenever the family doctor or the family lawyer comes on, wearing a pair of white spats, I am certain to guffaw right out. But one can not write humorously to any extent about a pair of white spats. The human interest is so soon exhausted.

Now with whiskers, it is different. Many of the best authorities regard whiskers as the funniest thing we have, on the stage or off. There are so many things to which whiskers can be compared. All varieties of whiskers are highly humorous, but some varieties are funnier than the others. I would grade them in the following order: Side-whiskers, especially white side-whiskers—subtle and refined humor; plain whiskers, including Vandykes and scrubby growths—tolerably funny; chin whiskers, particularly red ones, worn long and droopy —uproariously funny, mirth-provoking in the extreme, side-splitting.

Humorous writers derive a good deal of nourishment from whiskers. Calling a set of Vandykes a Lombardy poplar or a lignum-vitæ rarely fails to evoke laughter. Side-whiskers are mud-guards or biplanes or white wings or jib sails, depending upon their cut and color. Chin whiskers are feather dusters or Japanese airplants or paint brushes or impenetrable forests or No. 1 red winter wheat, or trailing arbutus, or what you will. By any other name a chin whisker would be as funny. It never fails.

Used in connection with a plug hat, it is absolutely irresistible.

I do not know why whiskers should be so humorous. From Adam down they have been the heritage of our sex. We should be used to them by this time. Yet a face be it ever so funny to look at in its shaven state, becomes funnier still to the public at large if left unshaven. I'll venture that there were several thousand voters in the state of New York who didn't vote for Charles Evans Hughes, the first time he ran for governor, because his picture made him look so much like a man climbing out of a fern dish. When the Republican National Convention in 1916 nominated Mr. Hughes for President, several million humorists, amateur and professional, simultaneously went "Ba-a-a!" like a goat, and the whole continent, from shore to shore, rocked with laughter; for Mr. Hughes, then as now, insisted on wearing his face full-rigged.

There are certain other things which both writers and comedians have found by testing to be almost as funny for general purposes as whiskers. Take eggs, now. All eggs are funny, but a fried egg is the most so. Scrambled eggs are only moderately funny, and there are persons who can control themselves at mention of a poached egg; but a hard-boiled egg is unfailing in its appeal to the risibilities, and a fried egg is a scream from start to finish, and from pit to dome. A cheese is always funny, whether written about, described, or exhibited. Limburger is the funniest brand, with Camembert next. Close behind cheese, and running it a close race in the popular favor as a humor asset, I would rate the onion. The lemon, which attained a sort of transient hold on the public fancy of late years, can never, in my opinion, hope to rival the onion as a permanent favorite. It lacks the drawing and holding qualities of the onion. After all, a lemon isn't near as funny, really, as a banana. But the onion is immortal; it is an epic; it is elemental humor. And so is cheese. *Semper Edam,* as the Latins said, signifying, "Always the cheese."

From the stern elderly onion of commerce, which dates back to the Old Red

Sandstone Period of Onions, on down to the young and comely spring onion, called in the North the scallion and in the South the shallot, all the known varieties of this succulent leek—the Bermuda onion, the Spanish onion, the mother of onion, the fried onion, the Little Neck onion on the half shell, the onion set, and the onion sprout—all hold high places in our national gallery of things that are innately humorous. To call a man an onion is very much funnier than calling him a radish, say, or a rutabaga, even though his resemblance to the last-named vegetable may be much greater than to an onion. I do not know why this should be so. The point remains that it is. And on the stage, well——

"Poor fellow, he leads a lonely life—nobody ever has anything to do with him."

"Why—is he a hermit?"

"No, he eats onions." (Gales of laughter.)

I always laugh at that one myself. And so it goes. A squash is moderately funny, and a string-bean is very funny indeed; but a green pea for some reason is not funny at all. A ham is funny, sausage is positively

uproarious, and fishballs are sort of laugh-
able; but a veal stew is regarded as possess-
ing few, if any, of the true elements of humor. Soup is still funny, but not as funny as
it was a few years back. Hash is immensely
humorous, but a croquette is not. Yet, what
is a croquette but hash that has come to a
head? A cow is funny, especially when
represented as having been mistaken for a
bull; but a bull, considered merely as a
bull, we do not laugh at.

Pie is simply excruciating in its powers
of humor. Custard pie is generally conceded to be the funniest pie we have, with
huckleberry pie coming second. Mince and
apple follow in the order named. Other
varieties of pie make up the field. One of
the funniest books that was ever written
took on added fun because its hero had the
same first name that a huckleberry pie has.

Of the human features, the nose is the
funniest, always excluding a head when it
is bald, a bald head being one of the funniest things that there are anywhere. The
Chinese, in their dramatic conceptions,
show a perverted idea of humor by painting

their comedians' noses white, whereas all
the civilized races know a nose is at its funniest when it is red. A nose is ever so much
funnier than an eye, even a black eye with
a patch over it; just as a leg is so much funnier than an arm that it is hardly worth
while to put an arm in the same category of
humor with a leg. In the degrees of humorous relationship, old maids rank first, then
mothers-in-law, and then elderly unmarried
uncles. I do not undertake to explain why
these things are. I only go by the rules as
laid down by the masters of the craft and
followed ever since by all their disciples.
A beginner who follows them can hardly
fail to turn out funny stuff.

Certain words, like certain names, are
exceedingly humorous. Perigee is a particularly funny word, and so is apogee, and
so, in fact, is almost every word which
sounds as if it had been put up on a curling-
iron. Nothing so helps along a whimsical
story about an animal or an insect, such as
a housefly or a pollywog or a catfish, as
calling it by its Latin name, especially if the
Latin name happens to be long and double-

jointed. Names of towns in which the letter K occurs are almost invariably funny. Take, for example, Kankakee, which is the funniest of them all, because the K occurs three times, and Keokuk and Kalamazoo. Poughkeepsie, on the other hand, is only moderately funny—the K comes so far back that it is practically smothered under a load of other consonants which lack the true humor touch.

From time to time attempts have been made to put Paducah prominently forward into the list of towns with funny names. These efforts have uniformly failed because Paducah suffers from the fatal defect of having no K in it. Spell it Paduky and the results might be different. The same may be said of Cohoes, which has also been entered several times, but without real success. It would seem, at a casual glance, that Q or Z should be a much funnier letter than K; but such is not the case. There are some things about our national humor that are past finding out.

Names of individuals are funnier when they suggest things. A long name like

Archibald Claveringhouse DeMontmoren-
cy Potts is naturally funny. It makes you
think of getting on the Twentieth Century
Limited and being put off at a flag station.
Similarly, one of those through vestibuled
names, such as J. Mozart Chatterton-Chat-
terton Hamiltonian-Wilkes Jones, is funny
because it is long enough to let the last half
run as a second section and still have enough
name left over to satisfy the wants of almost any ordinary person. But why should
Cadwallader be a funnier name than Van-
derbilt or Montgomery? It is, and I'm
sure I don't know why, and I've given the
subject considerable study.

These things are mostly the humor of in-
animate objects—what you might call still-
life humor. When we come to the humor
of action, of life, and of motion, undoubtedly the one funniest thing that is offered to
the consideration of mankind is a fat man
falling down on his own high hat and crush-
ing it beyond repair. Thin people are still
quite funny, especially very thin people
who look as though they might be suffering
from slow, wasting diseases, although not as

funny as they were back in the days of the
Early Victorian School of Humor, when
Dickens wrote about them and Cruikshank
drew them; but even in that period fat
people undoubtedly held the first place.

Personally, I used to think fat men were
funnier than I do now. It has been my experience that when a writer begins to fleshen
up a trifle himself; when he begins to wear
his figure at half mast and people who pass
him on the street in warm weather look at
his double chins and stop him and tell him
he's melting and running down on his
clothes; I say, when he reaches the stage of
what you might call—oh, no, not obesity;
nothing like that, I assure you—but merely
is what you might term pleasantly plump—
when he hesitates about renting a New York
flat for fear he might be taken with some in-
flammatory disease while residing therein,
which would necessitate the removal of a
side wall in order to get him to the hospital;
I repeat once again that when he reaches
this period he no longer regards jokes about
fat people with the same glee which filled

him on similar occasions in the days of his willowy, sylphlike youth.

But everybody else does. Everybody else is prepared to laugh at the sufferings of the man whose features have so merged into the background that his face has the appearance of having refused to jell, and who is trying to find a hat that will be becoming to him. A fat man is certainly a funny guy, as Henry James says in his "Life of the James Boys in Missouri."

A fat man falling down, just plain so, is funny. A fat man falling down on his hat is funnier still. A fat man falling down on his hat and breaking his umbrella, or a leg or something, is absolutely too funny for words. This is easy to understand when you come to think it over, because, in the final analysis, nearly all humor is founded on the idea of embarrassment or ridicule or suffering for somebody else. We don't laugh and grow fat; we laugh because other people grow fat. Seasickness is a remarkably humorous thing—when somebody else has it—and so is cramp-colic, or an abscessed tooth.

All of these things, though, are funnier on the stage, where you can see them, than they are in print, where you can only read about them—which brings me back to the point that the illustration is nearly always funnier than the text. Take comic artists, now.

On second thought, don't take comic artists. But consider the ridiculous ease of their calling as compared with that of their fellow-laborers who write. A comic artist draws an upright line crossed by several horizontal lines; that is a tree. Putting two candles and a few dewflickers on it makes it a Christmas tree. Putting a bulldog under it with the seat of a pair of small boy's trousers in its mouth makes an apple-tree—always a humorous study. The artist draws a jagged line across the paper like a first lesson in free-hand writing, and inserts in the middle a fat man in a bathing suit, holding up one foot, with a crab dangling from the big toe. Result—a highly humorous picture of the Atlantic Ocean.

To suggest late at night, he has only to draw a skyline—two chimneys, one gable roof, and a steeple, with a tom-cat on the gable, and behind the steeple either a new moon or a full moon—depending on whether it is easier for him to draw his moons while full, or otherwise—and there you have an awfully funny picture of half-past two o'clock in the morning. He thinks up a series showing, each Sunday, how the humorous Hausenpfeffer Twins commit mayhem, manslaughter, and other childish diversions on their aged and decrepit grandfather, in four colors, and it runs on for years and years, growing funnier all the time. If I couldn't be a high-salaried comedian, I should like to be a high-salaried comic artist—all the writing persons whom I have interviewed feel the same way about it that I do.

A really funny idea has a long, long life and a merry one. I've known funny ideas that had grown sixteen rattles and a button, and were still wagging along steadily. The joke lasts; it's the poor fellow who first thought it up that wears out. A humorist working by the day at Denver, Colorado, we will say, has a funny idea. It's a bully funny idea. It comes to him like a bolt from the blue. He's mooning along without a cloud in the sky, or a leaf stirring, and all of a sudden—bang! there is the idea sloshing around in his brain, making trouble for the old settler ideas that have been there all along. It is a noble and a precious and a priceless thing, and he figures he ought to get as much as seventy-five cents for it. So he clutches the new-born treasure to his bosom and runs to the office and commits it to paper while it's still pink and palpitating. An editor lances it in a vital spot with a pencil and drains a little of the life-blood out of it. A printer intersperses typographical errors here and there, where they will do the most harm. A proof-reader has his little fling at it, and finally, in a crippled but still attractive state, it sees the garish light of day, and takes its foot in its hand and starts on its travels.

A paragrapher in Houston packs it down into a line. A versifier in Duluth stretches it into a jingle and sells it to a comic weekly with a large tonsorial parlor and day coach circulation. The man who writes the syndicate theatrical letter for the Sunday papers turns it into a bit of repartee and says Wilton Lackaye said it at The Lambs' Club. By turns, it is an anecdote, a *bon mot,* an after-dinner speech, an end-man's means of visible support, a popular song, an apt retort, a catch line, a space filler, a movie subtitle, a set of verses, a slogan, and a parody.

Thus, by easy stages, it reaches New York. At first New York receives it dubiously, on the principle that anything worth happening at all would naturally have happened in New York in the first place. But, after due thought, Al H. Woods or the Shuberts decide that it is susceptible of a Broadway setting and would therefore make a good musical comedy. No sooner said than done; in fact, sometimes even sooner than that. They hire a comic opera librettist to write a book around it, which he does some morning right after breakfast. The Words and Music Brothers do the songs, and it runs for nine months in one theater and then goes on the road for two seasons, paying in royalties eighteen thousand dollars, which is exactly seventeen thousand, nine hundred and ninety-nine dollars and twenty-five cents more than the fellow out in Denver got.

But the end is not yet. In the meanwhile it has crossed the seas to the Mother Country, where, after being carefully sterilized, deodorized, searched for concealed deadly points, disinfected, and furnished with footnotes, a chart, a glossary, and a set of plans and specifications, it becomes a regular English joke and appears in *Punch*. It is then copied back on this side by the *Evening Post*. Nine years later the *Boston Transcript* prints it with a credit to *Harper's Weekly*. And then some hoary-headed old doodle-bug of an antiquarian crawls out from under a log in the woods and produces the proof to show that it was stolen from Charles Lamb, who got it from Aristophanes, who copied it from one of the Pyramids, but after that that its real origin is lost in the mists of prehistoric times.

For, when all is said and done, real humor is even as bread cast upon the waters—it returns to you after many days with somebody else's name signed to it.

THE END

Date Due